W9-AMJ-358

DIY *for* DOG LOVERS

DIY *for* DOG LOVERS

36 PAW-SOME CANINE CRAFTS

by Kat Roberts

LARK

New York

New York

An Imprint of Sterling Publishing Co., Inc.
1166 Avenue of the Americas
New York, NY 10036

LARK and the distinctive Lark Crafts logo are registered trademarks of Sterling Publishing Co., Inc.

Text © 2019 Kat Roberts
Cover and photography © 2019 Sterling Publishing Co., Inc.

All rights reserved. No part of this publication may be reproduced, stored in a retrieval system, or transmitted in any form or by any means (including electronic, mechanical, photocopying, recording, or otherwise) without prior written permission from the publisher.

ISBN 978-1-4547-1072-1

Distributed in Canada by Sterling Publishing Co., Inc.
c/o Canadian Manda Group, 664 Annette Street
Toronto, Ontario M6S 2C8, Canada
Distributed in the United Kingdom by GMC Distribution Services
Castle Place, 166 High Street, Lewes, East Sussex BN7 1XU, England
Distributed in Australia by NewSouth Books
University of New South Wales, Sydney, NSW 2052, Australia

For information about custom editions, special sales, and premium and corporate purchases, please contact Sterling Special Sales at 800-805-5489 or specialsales@sterlingpublishing.com.

Manufactured in China

2 4 6 8 10 9 7 5 3 1

larkcrafts.com
sterlingpublishing.com

Photography by Chris Bain
Interior design by Shannon Nicole Plunkett
Interior dog illustrations by Julia Morris

Contents

Introduction

My dog inspires me daily with her loyalty, humor, and love. Sharker greets me when I return home after work, always joyful. She can calm my nerves when I feel anxious or frazzled, and she always makes me smile, whatever my mood. No matter what I do, whether it's planning a party for kids, designing fashion for grown-ups, or creating useful home organizing and storage solutions, she remains front and center. She's a member of the family, and it's likely most of you feel the same way about your dogs.

If you love dogs and also love to craft, these projects will definitely fit the bill! I am very excited to share with you these thirty-six cute and clever doggie crafts, divided into five sections—home, accessories, fashion, entertaining, and canine gear for your dog.

This fun and lively book is all about making and having fun while celebrating our furry best friends. So thanks, Sharker, for all the love you've given me and for being the inspiration for this book. You're the baddest!

Getting Started: Techniques, Tips & Materials

HAND-STITCHING TECHNIQUES

For the most part, the sewing in this book is done by hand, though there are some projects that can be done with a sewing machine to save time. If you don't have a sewing machine, don't worry. You can get the same great results with hand sewing. Here is a list of basic stitches to use.

Running Stitch

Creating a Running Stitch couldn't be easier. Just go in and out through the materials while keeping even spacing in between each stitch.

Double Running Stitch

Double Running Stitch begins the same as the Running Stitch, but when you get to the end of the row, reverse direction, sewing back up to the top through the exact same holes. This fills in the spaces between the first row of stitches, resulting in a line that resembles the look of a sewing machine.

Whip Stitch

The Whip Stitch is a simple, decorative stitch that is created in much the same way as a Running Stitch. The only difference is that you will be going over the edge, making the stitch through the back to the front each time.

Double Whip Stitch

The Double Whip Stitch is a continuation of a standard Whip Stitch. Just like with the Double Running Stitch, when you get to the end of your row, reverse directions, sewing another Whip Stitch until you reach the point where you began.

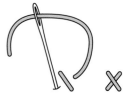

Criss-Cross Stitch

Criss-Cross Stitch is very similar to a traditional Cross-Stitch. Use an erasable fabric pen, pencil, or chalk to outline two parallel rows of dots. Starting with the bottom-left dot, bring the needle up through the fabric and stitch upward to the dot that's above and to the right. Your next stitch will come up through the bottom dot just beneath that top stitch. Repeat this process until you reach the right side. Now go from the bottom-left stitch up to the dot above and to the left. Repeat until you reach the left side. When you're finished, the stitches will look like Xs. To make a Double Criss-Cross Stitch, overlap two Criss-Cross Stitches at alternating angles.

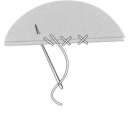

Chain Stitch

A Chain Stitch is an embroidery stitch where a series of stitches is linked together like a chain. To do this stitch, you will bring the threaded needle up through the fabric. Place the needle back into the same hole that you came out of, but bring the tip of the needle out again ⅛ inch (3 mm) away. Loop the thread around this needle tip before putting the needle all the way through the fabric. Continue repeating these steps to create a chain of stitches. This is a great stitch for outlining, creating letters, or filling an area of fabric.

French Knots

French Knots are a beautiful and easy-to-do decorative embroidery technique, and are used for the Embroidered Poodle Dog Patch on page 44. To do this stitch, bring your needle up through the surface of the fabric. Wrap the thread around the tip of the needle twice before putting the needle back through the fabric near the hole that you came out of.

Combination Stitches

Now that you know these basics, you can combine them for different looks. For example, layering a Double Running Stitch with a Running Stitch as seen in the Fido Phone Case (page 26) not only gives a great look but also provides added strength to the edge!

WORKING WITH TEMPLATES

There are a lots of templates used in this book. For best results, I suggest making a photocopy of the templates so you can keep the original in pristine shape—this also allows you to easily make any of the projects more than once. This is particularly handy if you are having a craft night with your friends!

MODIFYING TEMPLATES

Please keep in mind that dogs come in all shapes and sizes. In the projects for dogs, the important thing is that the craft is the right size and fit for *your* dog. You can and should make size modifications to the templates to best fit the needs of your dog by using a copy machine to shrink or enlarge any of the templates, or by tracing the template onto a large sheet of paper and making the modifications there.

TRANSFERRING DESIGNS

For some projects, you need to transfer a design onto your materials. There are a number of ways to do this. Below are three techniques. Use whichever seems to make the most sense for your specific project.

Light

Lay your material on top of the design template, and place both layers on a light box or against a brightly lit window. The light showing through should make your design visible enough to trace with an erasable fabric pen, pencil, or chalk.

Carbon Paper

Place a piece of carbon paper facedown on your material with the design placed faceup on top. Trace the design, either with a pencil or a tracing wheel. I'd suggest trying this on a scrap piece of fabric first to get the hang of it before working directly with your materials to ensure the markings are visible on the fabric, as well as making sure you are only leaving markings exactly where you need them.

Pinholes

Use an awl or straight pin to make a number of holes on the outlines of the design, piercing the paper. Place the template onto your fabric and color a dot over each of the holes with an erasable fabric pen, pencil, or chalk. When you pick up the paper, you will see the dots on the fabric indicating where your design will be.

PROTECT YOURSELF, PROTECT YOUR STUFF

Like most fun activities, crafting can sometimes get a bit messy. If your project involves glues, paints, or any kind of spray, it's best to make sure that you and your work areas are both covered. A simple smock and rubber gloves should take care of you, and butcher paper or old newspaper can safely cover your work surface—though be conscious of newspaper ink transferring onto fabrics. If you have a project that involves multiple colors of paint, I'd recommend keeping a few paper plates around for easy organizing and cleanup. And be sure that any projects using spray paint or spray adhesive are done outside, where you will have proper ventilation.

Most of the projects in this book are intended to be created by adults. While there are also plenty of fun and easy projects that can be done by children, they should be supervised during crafting. It's also important to note that using safe materials are a good idea not only for you but also for your dog. Nontoxic materials (glues, paints, etc.) are the way to go if they will be coming in contact with your pets.

YOU DO YOU

I think the best crafting projects are the ones that are most personal to *you*, so if you feel like adding more color, more prints, more rhinestones, more embroidery, or subtracting some—or all—of it, go right ahead! This is all about what appeals most to your aesthetic. And same goes for your dog! Mix colors, materials, whatever you like to reflect their personality. Have fun with it!

MATERIALS

Fabric

If you've ever stepped into a fabric store, then you know there are tons of different fabrics in every weight, texture, and print imaginable. The fabric projects in this book don't require anything fancy, so feel free to grab a fabric that you are most drawn to. However, it's a good practice when fabric-shopping to have your future creation in mind.

Felt

The affordability, vibrancy, and ease of working with felt are just a few of the reasons it's such a popular and fantastic crafting material, but be aware that all felt is not created equally. Some felt is extremely flimsy or lacking in strength. It doesn't have to be super thick or the most expensive option, but quality matters. The better your felt, the nicer and more durable your finished project is likely to be!

Card Stock

Card stock is paper that is a bit thicker than a regular sheet of paper, which gives it a little more strength. For any project in this book requiring card stock, you are welcome to use a manila folder or index card, but there are lots of great paper stores that offer card stock in a wide variety of color, prints, and finishes. These stores can be a wonderful resource for tailoring the projects to your specific taste.

Embellishments

You'll notice that some of the projects in these pages use embellishments. My favorites are sequins, rhinestones, and other shiny beads. If these don't fit with your aesthetic, feel free to substitute an embellishment that is more to your taste. Going rogue is always encouraged!

Home

A house just isn't a home without dogs . . . lots and lots of dogs!
Give your living space a touch of canine class with
these pooch-inspired projects.

Silhouette Art

Embrace your shadow side! This project gives an old-school Victorian art form a majorly modern, dog-friendly upgrade!

What You Need:

Pencil

Templates (see page 91)

Black paper

Scissors

Variety of small frames,
2½ × 3½ inches (6.4 × 8.9 cm),
2 × 2 inches (5.1 × 5.1 cm),
one for every silhouette you
create

White paper

Glue stick

What You Do:

1. Trace your templates onto the black paper (A).

2. Very slowly and carefully, cut each of them out. Be sure to pay extra attention to the details (B).

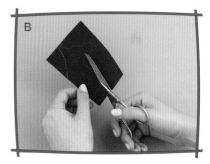

3. Use the glass within the frame as a template by tracing its outline onto the white paper. This will give you accurate dimensions for each frame's interior (C).

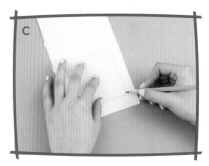

4. Cover the wrong side of the cut-out dogs with glue.

5. Stick each dog to one of the white pieces of paper (D).

6. Place the artwork in the frame, and hang or display in a small grouping.

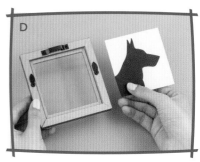

Pomeranian Mug

The next time you're dog-tired, let this cute mug be the cheerful bearer of your coffee!

What You Need:

Scrap paper (optional)

Permanent marker, black

Porcelain mug

Rubbing alcohol and cotton swabs (optional)

Oven

Tip: Before you start drawing on the mug, take a moment to practice drawing a dog or two on the scrap paper (A, B). These Pomeranians are very easy to draw, but practice makes perfect!

What You Do:

1. With the permanent marker, draw dash marks in a circle on your mug to create the dog's head (C).

2. For the ears, draw two triangles with smaller triangles within them (D).

3. Draw in simple facial features: eyes, nose, mouth, whiskers, and tongue. Variety in the dogs' faces is strongly encouraged (E). Have fun with it!

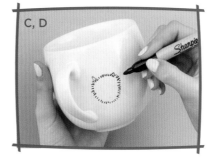

Tip: Keep some rubbing alcohol and a few cotton swabs on hand in case you make a mistake or want to redraw a feature. To remove markings, simply apply some rubbing alcohol to the tip of a cotton swab and wipe the mark you want to remove. Allow a few moments to thoroughly dry before redrawing.

4. Once you have finished drawing on the outside of the mug, it needs to bake in the oven to make the markings permanent. Preheat your oven to 300°F. Place the mug on a cookie sheet and the cookie sheet in the oven. Let bake for 1 hour.

5. After 1 hour, turn off the oven. Leave the mug inside the oven until it has cooled down, a few hours.

Note: For best results, the mug should be washed by hand with a soft sponge and not put in the dishwasher.

Paw Prints
Rolling Pin Stamp

Because this fun stamp lets you cover a lot of space quickly, it is ideal for printing on large surfaces. It's particularly good for making your own paw print wrapping paper or fabric yardage.

What You Need:

Pen

Templates (page 92)

Adhesive-backed foam sheets,
    8½ × 5½ inches (21.6 × 14 cm)

Scissors

Rolling pin

Paintbrush

Paint

Paper or fabric (for printing on)

Scrap paper

Hot glue (optional)

Note: Most adhesive-backed foams are perfect for this project, but if you notice your adhesive is not as strong as it needs to be to keep the shapes on, you can attach them with a thin layer of hot glue.

What You Do:

1. Use a pen to trace each part of the paw print templates onto the right side of the foam (A). You will need approximately 25 of each shape.

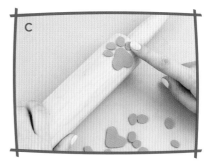

2. Carefully cut them out (B).

3. Remove the adhesive backs and begin assembling the paws on the surface of the rolling pin (C).

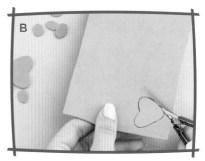

4. When you've finished covering the rolling pin, use the paintbrush to add a thin layer of paint to each of the paws (D).

5. Lay the rolling pin down on the surface that you would like to print, and roll with even pressure.

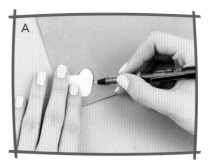

6. Add more paint as needed.

7. When you are done, remove the extra paint by rolling the pin on a piece of scrap paper until it no longer makes marks.

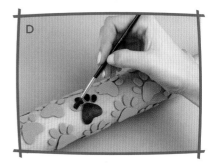

"All You Need is Love . . . & Dogs" Banner

The Beatles were half right when they famously sang "All You Need is Love."

What You Need:

Iron

Fabric measuring 12¼ × 19¾ inches (31 × 50 cm) (make sure to leave ½-inch seam allowance)

Templates (page 93)

Erasable fabric pen, pencil, or chalk

Scissors

Sewing machine

Sewing thread

Stiffened felt, 8½ × 11 inches (21.6 × 27.9 cm) in black

Small scissors

Clear, gridded ruler

Fabric glue

Dowel rod, 12 inches long (30.5 cm) and approx. XX in diameter

Raffia, cord, or yarn for hanging, 18 inches (45.7 cm)

What You Do:

1. Iron the fabric.

2. Trace the banner template onto the wrong side of the fabric and cut out (A).

3. Place right-side down, then fold all of the edges back ½ inch (1.3 cm) and iron flat (B).

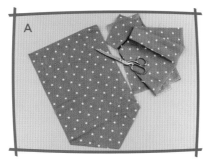 

4. Turn right-side up, then, using the sewing machine, sew around all sides, ¼ inch (6 mm) away from the edge (C).

5. At the top edge of the banner, fold over 1 inch (2.5 cm), then sew straight across (D).

 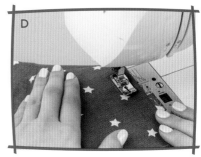

6. Trace each of the letter and punctuation templates onto the wrong side of the stiffened felt.

7. Use the small pair of scissors to cut out each letter and punctuation mark **(E)**.

8. Find the placement for the first two words by using the clear, gridded ruler to measure 2 inches down from the stitched line across the banner's top. The words *ALL YOU* will be placed here **(F)**.

9. Double-check that the letters are aligned the way you like and then adhere them with the fabric glue.

10. Measure 1 inch (2.5 cm) down from the row of text, then begin placing the next two words, *NEED IS*. When you're satisfied with the position of the words, adhere with glue.

11. Measure 1 inch (2.5 cm) down and then add *LOVE . . .* Check placement and then glue.

12. Again, measure down 1 inch (2.5 cm) to add the last two words, *& DOGS*, and then glue **(G)**.

13. Slide the dowel rod into the pocket at the top of the banner.

14. On either side of the dowel rod, attach the raffia with a slipknot **(H)**.

15. Hang and enjoy!

Bone-Shaped Welcome Mat

No bones about it, this simple project will be a canine complement to your mudroom or doorway.

What You Need:

White pencil or chalk

Template (page 92)

Door mat, made of coir or jute and rubber-backed, 18 × 30 inches (45.7 × 76.2 cm)

Heavy-duty scissors

What You Do:

1. Using the pencil or chalk, trace the template onto the wrong side of the mat (A).

2. Using the scissors, cut directly on the line (B).

3. When you've finished, turn right side up to check that the bone shape looks right. Snip away any areas that appear misshapen (C).

Note: Depending on what materials the doormat is made from, this project can get quite messy. Do your cutting in an outside area, if possible, where the mess can be easily swept up.

Decoupage Treat Jar

This doggie treat jar is a great way to store your pet's snacks. Customize this project with a humorous picture of your dog. Best of all, the decoupage medium creates a textured surface that can be easily wiped clean.

What You Need:

Photo of your dog

Scissors

Double-stick tape

Glass jar with lid

Paintbrush

Decoupage medium

What You Do:

1. When choosing a photo of your dog, pick one with a solid-colored background (this will make cutting out your dog easier) **(A)**. Cut out the photo of your dog so that none of the background remains **(B)**.

2. Cover the back of the photo with double-stick tape **(C)**. None of the tape should be seen from the front, so trim away any that is visible.

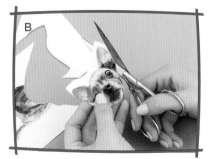
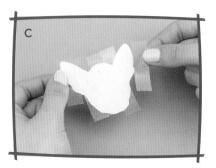

3. Center the photo on the jar, about halfway from the top.

4. Use the paintbrush to begin covering the photo and the rest of the jar with decoupage medium, avoiding the jar's interior and bottom **(D)**. Allow at least 20 minutes to dry, but refer to manufacturer's instructions for exact drying time.

5. Add a second coat **(E)** and allow at least 20 minutes to dry, referring to manufacturer's instructions.

> *Note: This jar can be cleaned with a soft sponge, but before cleaning for the first time, allow for appropriate curing time*

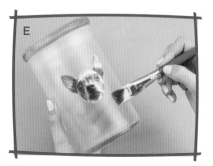

Handy Leash Holder

Don't get stuck looking for the leash when your pet has got to go! Hang this leash holder right next to the door so you're always ready when they are.

What You Need:

Wooden plaque, 5 × 7 inches (12.7 × 17.8 cm)

Wood stain, in white

Clear, gridded ruler

Pencil

Patterning tape, ⅛ inches width (3 mm) and ¼ inches (6 mm) width

Small paintbrush

Acrylic paint, in eggshell and robin's-egg blue

Template (page 95)

Adhesive vinyl, 4 × 3½ inches, in white (10.2 × 8.9 cm)

Screwdriver

Two-prong hook, 2¾ inches (7 cm) width

Wood screws

Wall hook

Hammer

What You Do:

1. Paint the front and sides of the plaque with the white stain. Wipe off excess stain after 30 seconds to 1 minute **(A)**.

2. Repeat step 1 until you've achieved the desired opacity. Allow at least 1 hour to dry.

3. Use the clear, gridded ruler and the pencil to measure and draw a vertical line down the center of the plaque **(B)**.

4. Draw a diagonal line from the left-hand side of the plaque to the centerline.

5. Repeat step 4, this time on the right-hand side of the plaque.

6. Place a piece of the ⅛-inch (3 mm) tape just beneath the diagonal lines on each side. Make sure the two pieces form a clean-looking point at the center where they overlap **(C)**.

7. Measure ½ inch down from the bottom edge of the tape, and draw a diagonal line on the left and right sides.

8. Place a piece of the ¼-inch tape just beneath the diagonal lines on each side. Again, make sure the two pieces create a clean-looking point at the center where they overlap.

9. Measure ¼ inch (6 mm) down from the bottom edge of the tape, and draw a diagonal line on the left and right sides.

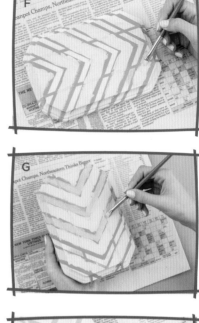

10. Repeat steps 6 through 9 until you reach the bottom of the plaque **(D)**.

11. Draw a vertical line down the plaque 1 inch away from the center line on both the left and right sides.

12. Cover each with ⅛-inch (3 mm) width tape **(E)**.

13. Use the paintbrush to fill in all of the ½-inch (1.3 cm) spaces with the eggshell-colored paint. Clean the brush **(F)**.

14. Paint in all of the ¼ inch (6 mm) spaces with the robin's-egg-blue paint **(G)**.

15. Remove all of the tape before the paint has completely dried **(H)**.

16. Trace all of the template pieces on the vinyl and cut out.

17. Once the paint has dried, remove the adhesive backing from the vinyl pieces and place on the top half of the plaque.

18. Beneath the paw print, use the screwdriver to secure the hook to the plaque **(I)**.

19. Finish by using the hammer to add the wall hanger on the backside of the plaque.

Labradoodle Pillow

The next time you're vegging out on the sofa, let this fluffy new friend join you.

What You Need:

Erasable fabric marker, pencil, or pen

Templates (pages 94–95)

Faux fur, 13 × 30 inches (33 × 76.2 cm) in white

Felt, 1½ × 1½ inches (3.8 × 3.8 cm) in brown

Scissors

Straight pins

Sewing machine

Sewing needle

White thread

Polyester-fiber filling

2 cotton pom-poms, 1 inch (2.5 cm) in black

Fabric glue

What You Do:

1. With your erasable fabric marker, trace 2 of template 1 and 4 of template 2 onto the faux fur. Trace the nose template onto the felt once. Cut all of them out **(A)**.

2. Pin each of the ear pairs together with right sides facing, as pictured **(B)**.

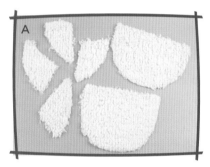 

3. Using a sewing machine, sew from the left side all the way around to the right side. Do not sew the flat bottom **(C)**.

4. Flip right-side out **(D)**.

 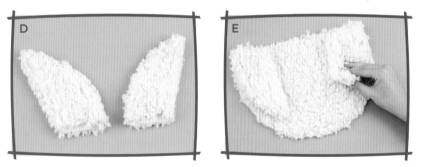

5. Place the ears onto one of the larger pieces of faux fur, as pictured. The flat edges are flush, but each ear is placed ⅜ inch (9.5 cm) away from the rounded outer edge of the faux fur **(E)**.

6. Cover with the remaining piece of faux fur, with the right side facing down. Pin together.

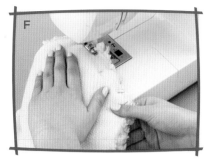

7. Double Running Stitch all around, sewing ¼ inch (6 mm) away from the edge, leaving a 3-inch (7.6 cm) opening on the curved bottom (F).

8. Flip right-side out.

9. Fill with the polyester-fiber filling (G), then hand-stitch the bottom opening closed with a Double Running Stitch. Be sure to fold the raw edges inward before sewing so they are not visible on the finished pillow (H).

10. Fold the ears down so that each side looks symmetrical, and hand-stitch into place with a couple of Double Running Stitches (I).

11. Hand-stitch each pom-pom to the front, then glue down the felt nose with fabric glue, as pictured (J).

Blue Dog Frame

This quick and easy project is the perfect way to dress up a plain wooden frame.

What You Need:

Wooden frame, 4 × 6 inches (10.2 × 15.2 cm)

Spray paint

Dog figurine, 2 inches (5 cm)

Glue gun

What You Do:

1. Remove the glass from the frame.

2. Spray paint the frame and the figurine (A), and allow at least 20 minutes to dry. (Check manufacturer's instructions for exact drying times.)

3. Apply glue to the bottom right-hand side of the frame (B), and adhere the figurine to it (C).

4. Add a favorite photo, then attach the glass to the frame.

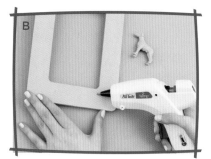
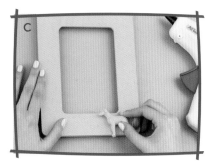

Accessories

Make a statement with these cute little projects, which will definitely put some pooch in your day-to-day routine.

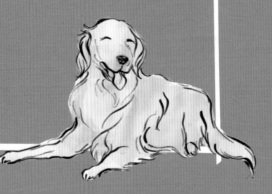

Pink Poodle Journal

Jot down notes in style with this flowery poodle journal.

What You Need:

Pencil

Template (page 96)

Card stock, 6½ × 5½ inches
(16.5 × 14 cm) in light pink

Scissors

Craft glue

Paper flowers, 1 inch (2.5 cm)
in yellow

Permanent marker, in black

Journal, 7 × 10 inches
(17.8 × 25.4 cm) in pink

What You Do:

1. Trace the template onto the card stock and cut out (A).

2. Glue the paper flowers onto the card stock as pictured (B).
Allow at least 20 minutes to dry.

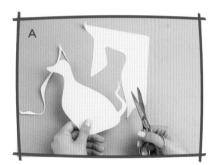

3. Draw an eye and nose onto the card stock with your marker
to make a dog.

4. Spread glue in a thin, even layer onto the back of the card
stock.

5. Place the dog onto the
bottom right-hand side of
the journal (C). Press firmly,
but try to prevent any of
the glue from being visible
on the front of the journal.
Allow at least 20 minutes
to dry before using.

Fido Phone Case

Let this guard dog protect your phone!
The pattern can be customized for whatever size phone you have.

What You Need:

Pencil

Paper

Ruler

Scissors

Heavyweight felt, 10 × 8 inches (25.4 × 20.3 cm) in gray

Templates (page 96)

Erasable fabric pen, pencil, or marker

Medium-weight felt, 7 × 7 inches (17.8 × 17.8 cm) in light gray; 4 × 3 inches (10.2 × 7.6 cm) in black; and 1 × 1½ inches (2.5 × 3.8 cm) in pink

Embroidery floss, one skein each in black and white

Sewing needle

Fabric-covered button, ½ inch (1.3 cm) in black

Glue gun

Wiggly eyes, ¾ inch (1.9 cm)

straight pins

Sewing machine

Sewing thread in gray

What You Do:

1. Trace the outline of your phone onto a sheet of paper (A).

2. Measure the width of your phone.

3. Add half the width around the bottom and two sides of your tracing. Do not add anything to the top (B).

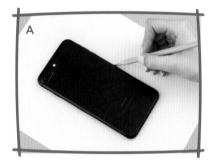
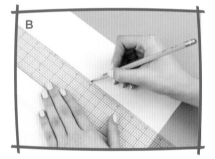

4. Now add an additional ¼ inch (6 mm) around the bottom and two sides (C).

5. Cut out this piece of paper. This will serve as your pattern.

6. Trace the pattern twice on the heavyweight gray felt and cut out (D).

7. Use the provided templates to trace the rest of the pieces onto the other pieces of felt, and cut them out as well.

8. Draw a 1-inch (2.5 cm) circle in the top-left quadrant of one of the heavyweight gray pieces of felt, as pictured (E).

9. With the black embroidery floss and sewing needle, hand-sew around the circle you drew in step 8 using a Double Running Stitch (F).

10. Add the pieces for the muzzle and tongue, as pictured. Then, with the white embroidery floss and sewing needle, hand-sew using a Running Stitch, as pictured (G). Finish by sewing the fabric button over the muzzle with black embroidery floss and sewing needle.

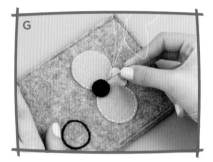

11. Use a glue gun to attach the 2 eyes, as shown (H).

12. Pin the two heavyweight gray pieces of felt. On the sewing machine, stitch them together around the two sides and the bottom (I).

13. Finish by stitching on the two ears with the black embroidery floss and needle, using a Running Stitch (J).

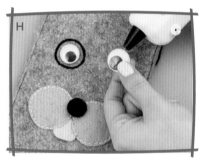

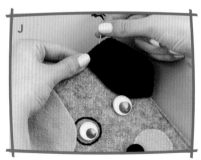

Note: Adjust the sizing of the provided templates to different-size phones in order to get a well-proportioned dog's face.

Man's Best Friendship Bracelet

This classic macramé project is the perfect way to declare your love for your furry best friends.

What You Need (per bracelet):

Scissors

Hemp cording, 6 feet (1.8 m)

Clipboard or tape

Round alphabet beads, ¼ inch (6 mm) in gold

Ruler

What You Do:

1. Cut the cording into three strands that are each 2 feet (24 in) long.

2. Secure the ends by tying an overhand knot approximately 1 inch (2.5 cm) from the top edge, then place the strands under a clipboard or tape to a sturdy surface to keep in place while you are doing the macramé work.

3. Braid the first 2 inches (5.1 cm) of the strands and then secure in another overhand knot (A).

4. Spread out the three strands.

5. Now lay the strand on the left over the center strand. The strand on the right should go under the center strand and over the strand on the left (B).

6. Take the end of the left-hand strand and put it under the right-hand strand (C).

7. Pull both ends, and it will tighten around the center strand. Continue to pull until tight (D).

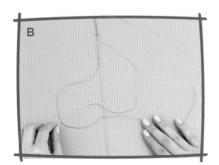

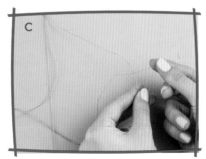

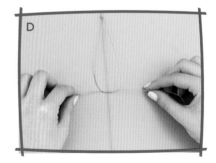

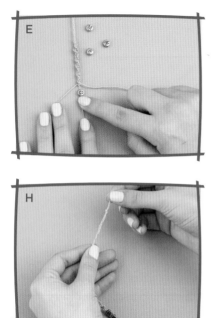

8. Repeat steps 5 through 7 until you have added another 2 inches (5.1 cm) of length to the bracelet.

9. With the beads, add the first letter of your dog's name to the strand in the middle **(E)**.

10. Repeat steps 5 through 7, then add the next letter **(F)**.

11. Continue until your dog's name has been spelled out.

12. Repeat steps 5 through 7 to add 2 inches (5.1 cm) of macramé **(G)**.

13. Finish by adding an overhand knot, then 1 inch (2.5 cm) of braid and another overhand knot **(H)**.

14. Trim the ends about ½ inch (6 mm) away from the final knot.

15. Your bracelet is ready to wear. Fasten the bracelet to your wrist by tying a knot with the two ends.

Dachshund Shopping Tote

This handy bag will show everyone around that you "totes" love your dogs!

What You Need:

Erasable fabric pen, pencil, or chalk

Templates (page 97)

Iron-on vinyl, 5½ × 12 inches (14 × 30.5 cm) in metallic silver; and 5½ × 12 inches (14 cm × 30.5 cm) in metallic gold

Scissors

Canvas tote bag, 13 × 13 inches (33 × 33 cm) in gray or your desired color

Scrap fabric

Iron

Ruler

What You Do:

1. Start by tracing your templates onto the wrong side of the silver and gold vinyl. In silver, you will need four left-facing dogs and two right-facing dogs. In gold, you will need four right-facing dogs and two left-facing dogs.

2. Cut them all out (A).

3. Start at the top left-hand side of the bag by placing a gold right-facing dog 1¼ inch (3.2 cm) away from the top of the bag. Use the ruler to ensure that the dog is straight (B).

4. Gently place scrap fabric over the dog and iron down (C). Double-check that the dog is well adhered. If not, iron again.

5. Now move to the top right-hand side of the bag, again using a right-facing gold dog. Use the ruler to line up the feet of the dog on the left-hand side with this right-hand side dog (D). Iron with the fabric over it.

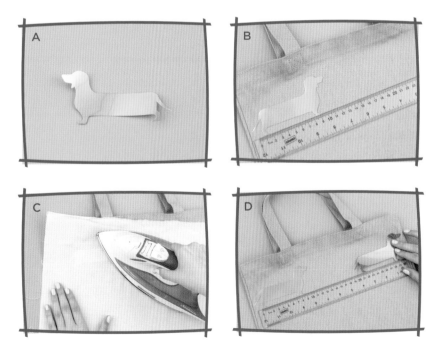

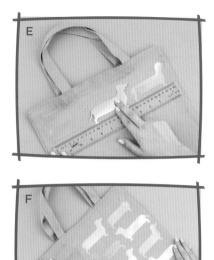

6. In between the two gold dogs, place a left-facing silver dog.

7. After making sure its feet are in alignment with the other two dogs **(E)**, cover with scrap fabric and iron.

8. Begin the next row of dogs ⅜ inch (9.5 cm) below. Start on the left-hand side, with a left-facing silver dog. After checking that it is straight, cover with scrap fabric and iron.

9. Now place another left-facing silver dog on the right-hand side. Check the alignment of the feet, then cover with scrap fabric and iron.

10. Place a left-facing gold dog between them, cover with scrap fabric, and iron.

11. Repeat steps 3 through 10.

12. When all dogs are on the bag, cover the whole thing with the scrap fabric and make one final pass with the iron **(F)**.

Color Block Dalmatian Shoes

Bold color blocking pairs with natural Dalmatian patterning in these impactful shoes that are sure to get you spotted!

What You Need:

Acrylic paint in black and green

Paintbrush

Shoes, made from canvas, faux leather, or leather, in white

Clear sealant (optional)

Tip: The spots should be asymmetrical, oblong shapes. The more you vary the marks, the more they will read as Dalmatian print. If you need help getting started, use the templates for the Lotsa Spots Jeans (page 42), or look at photos of Dalmatians.

What You Do:

1. Use black paint to make small, irregular black spots on the shoes (A).

2. Allow at least 30 minutes to dry.

3. Paint the back portion of the shoe in green paint (B). Allow at least 36 hours to dry before wearing.

   Note: It may take 2 to 3 coats of paint for the color to appear opaque, depending on the paint you are using.

4. As an optional, final step, you can paint a clear sealant over the painted areas of the shoe to protect the painted design.

Canine Clutch

Fetch all of your necessities from this unique, whimsical clutch.

What You Need:

Templates (page 98)

Erasable fabric pen, pencil, or chalk

Vinyl, 9½ × 20 inches (24.1 × 50.8 cm) in black; 5 × 6 inches (12.7 × 15.2 cm) in white

Scissors

Hook-and-loop tape, ¾ × 5 inches (1.9 × 12.7 cm) in black

Acrylic paint in black and aqua

Paintbrush

Craft glue

Sewing machine

Sewing thread, in black

What You Do:

1. Start by tracing your templates onto the wrong side of the vinyl.

2. Cut them all out.

3. Cut the hook-and-loop-tape into 4 pieces, each measuring ¾ × 1¼ inches (1.9 × 3.18 cm).

4. Paint the iris and pupil onto the small white vinyl pieces, as shown (A). Allow at least 30 minutes to dry.

5. Glue the nose to the muzzle.

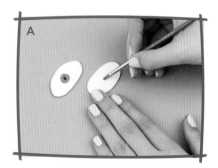

6. Now glue the eyes and muzzle to one of the large pieces of black vinyl (B), and allow at least 30 minutes for the glue to dry.

7. Following the placement indicated on the template, use a sewing machine to sew the hook-and-loop tape onto the piece of vinyl with the facial features on it (C).

8. Line up the two large pieces of vinyl and sew together on the sewing machine. The stitches should follow the path indicated on the template (D).

9. To close, push the ears down so that the pieces of hook-and-loop tape adhere (E).

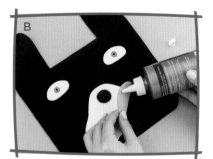

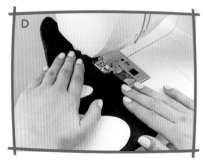

Fashion

Wear your dog on your sleeve—or your shirt, pants, or dresses!
This canine cache of projects is full of personality and
will add fun and style to your wardrobe.

Dog Lover's Anthem T-shirt

Sometimes being covered in your pet's hair is just a way of life.
Own it with this cheeky tee.

What You Need:

Iron

T-shirt

Clear, gridded ruler

Scrap of fabric

Scissors

Iron-on flocked letters,
    1½ inches (3.8 cm)
    in height

What You Do:

1. Iron your shirt flat.

2. Use your clear, gridded ruler to measure 2 inches (5.1 cm) down from the neck **(A)** and begin placing the cut-out letters to spell the words *DOG HAIR* onto the shirt with the plastic covering faceup **(B)**.

3. Use the ruler to measure 1¼ inches (3.2 cm) down from the words you just placed and add *DON'T CARE*, again making sure that the plastic is facing up.

4. Very carefully cover the letters with a piece of fabric scrap before ironing down **(C)**.

5. Repeat step 4.

6. Double-check that the letters are firmly secured to the shirt. Iron a bit longer if needed.

7. Remove the plastic covering from each of the letters **(D)**.

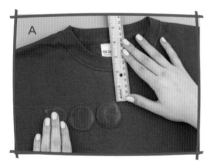

Tip: Because many iron-on alphabets don't include punctuation, you may need to make it yourself. Simply cut the apostrophe shape from one of the letters that you won't be using.

Lotsa Spots Jeans

Looking positively festive, you'll have no trouble being spotted
in these cute Dalmatian-print jeans!

What You Need:

Pen, pencil, or marker

Templates (page 97)

Iron-on flocked vinyl sheet,
12 × 12 inches
(30.5 × 30. 5 cm)

Scissors

White jeans

Scrap fabric

Iron

What You Do:

1. Trace each template onto the vinyl sheet approximately 30 times. You may need more or less depending on the size of the jeans (A).

2. Cut them out.

3. Place the cut pieces of flocking onto the front of the jeans with the plastic covering facing up. Vary the shapes placed around one another as much as possible (B).

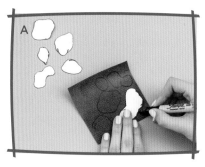

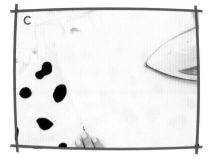

4. Place the piece of scrap fabric over the jeans and flocked shapes.

5. Iron the shapes onto the jeans (C). Follow the manufacturer's instruction on your package of flocking as to how long each piece will need to be ironed.

6. Once you've finished ironing, lift off the fabric to check that each piece has properly adhered to the surface of the jeans, paying extra attention to the outer edges.

7. Repeat steps 4 and 5 on any pieces that did not properly adhere the first time.

8. Repeat steps 3 through 7 on the backside of the jeans.

9. Carefully remove all of the plastic covering from the flocking (D).

Embroidered Dog Patches

Use beautiful but so-easy-to-do embroidery techniques to create these sew-on patches.
Two popular breeds, Boston terrier and poodle, will get you started,
but feel free to try your hand at other breeds as well.

What You Need:

Erasable fabric pen, pencil, or marker

Template (page 99)

Heavyweight canvas fabric,
4 × 8 inches (10.2 × 20.3 cm)

Embroidery thread, 1 skein each
in pink, light pink, hot pink,
black, and white

Embroidery needle

2 sequins, ¼ inch (6 mm)
in green

Pinking shears

What You Do:

BOSTON TERRIER PATCH

1. Transfer the design template onto your canvas.

2. Fill in all areas of color with a Chain Stitch (page XX). Start
with the black **(A)** and then fill in the white and the pink **(B)**.

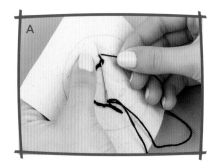 

3. Attach each sequin by bringing the needle up through the
center, and making a French knot (page x), before going
back through the center.

POODLE PATCH

1. Transfer the design template onto your canvas.

2. Start by filling in the face with a Chain Stitch in light
pink **(C)**.

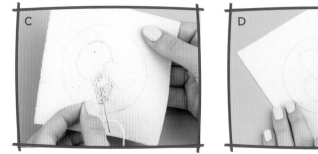 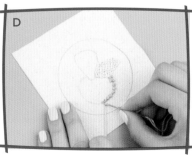

3. Next fill in the two other areas with French knots—use pink on the top of the head and hot pink for the ears **(D)**.

4. Add the facial details in black embroidery thread **(E)**.

5. For both patches, finish by cutting around the circle with pinking shears **(F)**.

6. Use a Running Stitch around the perimeter of the circle to attach to your clothing or a bag.

Paw Print Elbow Patches

These paw print elbow patches are a lighthearted and modern twist on a classic look.

What You Need:

Erasable fabric marker, pen, or chalk

Templates (page 99)

Scissors

Wool felt, 5 × 10 inches (12.7 × 25.4 cm) and ¼-inch (6 mm) thick in light brown

Sweater

Tape

Pins

Small notebook or cardboard

Sewing needle

Sewing thread in light brown

What You Do:

1. Trace two of each template in the felt, then cut out (A).

2. Put the sweater on and use a piece of tape to mark the placement of your left elbow (B). Take off the sweater.

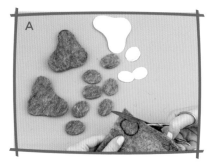

3. Place the felt pieces for the first paw over that spot, then remove the tape (C).

4. Pin down all of the pieces, making sure you don't pin through both sides of the sleeve (D).

5. Slide a very small notebook, piece of cardboard, or your phone into the sleeve, beneath the location of the felt pieces. (This will prevent you from accidentally sewing the sleeve shut.)

6. Using the needle and thread, sew all around each of the five felt pieces with a Running Stitch (E). Then remove the notebook from the sleeve.

7. Place the sleeves side by side, then place the wool pieces on the right sleeve so that they are perfectly lined up to the patches on the left side.

8. Repeat steps 4 through 6.

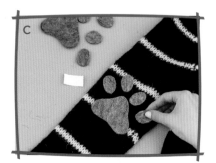

Chihuahua Appliqué Dog Pocket

Bring some unmistakable canine couture to your wardrobe with this cute appliqué pocket.

What You Need:

Erasable fabric marker, pencil, or pen

Templates (page 100)

Vinyl, 9½ × 8 inches (24.1 × 20.3 cm) in pale pink; 3 × 5 inches (7.6 × 12.7 cm) in black

Scissors

Transfer tape

Sewing needle

Sewing thread, black

Dress

Pins

What You Do:

1. Trace each template onto the vinyl, as indicated, and cut out **(A)**.

2. Place transfer tape on the back of the black piece of vinyl, then stick them to the pink piece of vinyl, as pictured **(B)**.

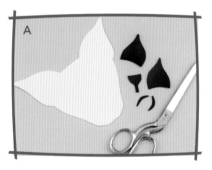
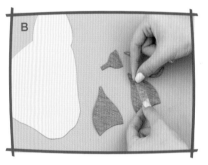

3. Stitch all of these pieces in place with a running stitch **(C)**.

4. Try on the dress and decide where you would like the pocket placed. Mark this area by pinning the pocket to the dress where you would like the center-top of the dog's head to be.

5. Place the vinyl on the dress, in the area indicated by the pin.

6. Stitch from the top of the left ear, around the outer portion of the head, and up to the top right ear with a Double Running Stitch **(D)**. Do not stitch at the top of the head so it may be used as a pocket.

Painted Pups Stenciled Shirt

Transform a plain button-down shirt into a major fashion statement with this multicolor stenciling project. What a dif-fur-ence some dogs make!

What You Need:

Pencil

Templates (page 101)

Large pieces of paper

Small scissors

Cardboard (a piece as large as your shirt)

Button-down cotton broadcloth shirt, in white

Fabric spray paint in pink, yellow, green, orange, and aqua

Permanent fabric marker in black

Scrap fabric

Iron

What You Do:

1. Trace the template onto one of the large sheets of paper.

2. Because you are creating a stencil, you will need to keep the paper intact, cutting away only the interior area of the templates, as pictured (A).

3. To make sure the cardboard will fit snugly inside of the shirt, place your shirt on top of the cardboard and trace around it.

4. Cut away the excess cardboard.

5. Place the cardboard inside the shirt (B). This will keep the paint from soaking through to the back of the shirt.

6. Place the template over the shirt. If any areas of fabric stick out from the sides, cover with pieces of paper to protect them from the paint.

7. Start spraying one color at a time over each of the cutouts (C). Just a few sprays will do; you can always go back and add more color if needed.

8. Repeat step 7 with all of the colors (D).

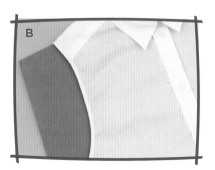

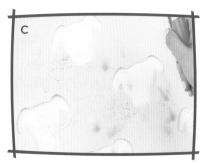

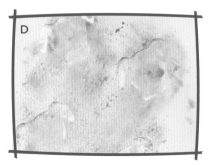

9. When you have finished, remove the stencil and other pieces of paper. Allow plenty of time to dry.

10. Draw simple faces onto each of the dogs with the fabric marker (E, F) and let dry.

   Optional: If you would like the design to appear on the back of the shirt as well, repeat steps 5 through 10 once the front of the shirt has dried.

11. Remove the cardboard from inside of the shirt.

12. Cover the shirt with the scrap fabric and iron.

Note: *Shirt should be allowed to dry for at least 72 hours before cleaning. Always wash inside out.*

Entertaining

You'll want to craft all of these dog-themed decorations for your next party. They're fun, festive, and so easy to make.

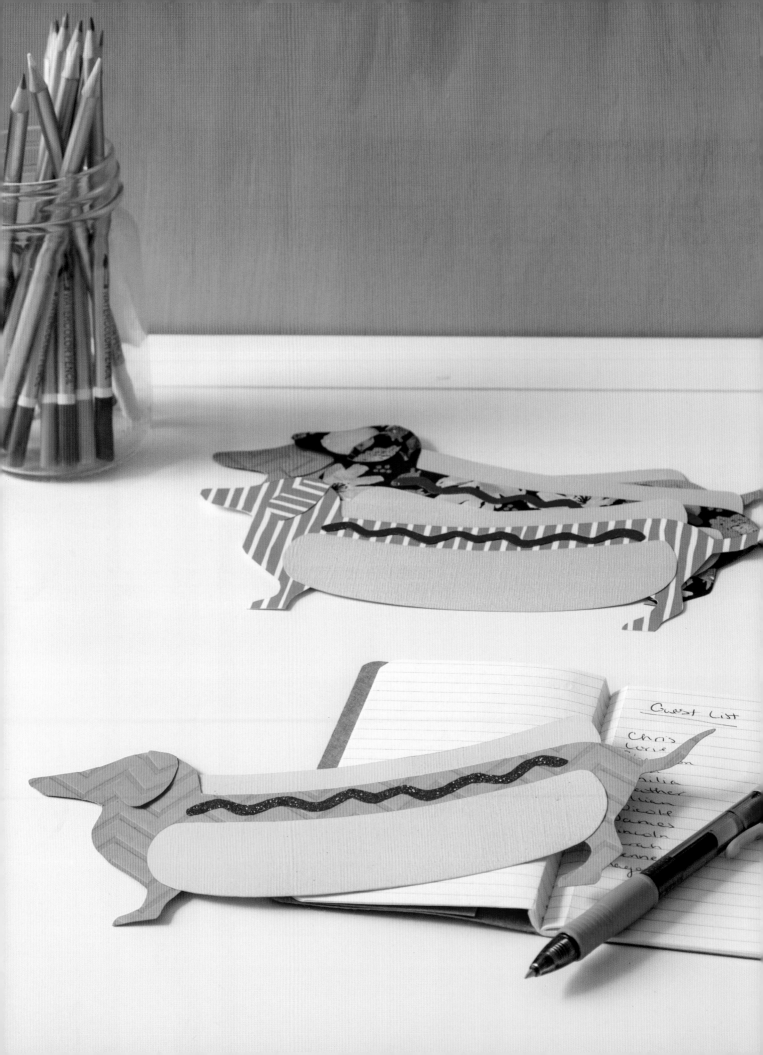

Wiener Dog Invitations

Hot dog, you're having a party! Let these funny invites set the tone for the big event.

What You Need (per invite):

Pencil

Scissors

Templates (page 102)

Card stock, 4 × 10 inches (10.2 × 25.4 cm) in hot pink, 6½ × 6½ inches (16.5 × 16.5 cm) in yellow, 5 × ½ inch (12.7 × 1.3 cm) in red glitter

Red marker

Glue stick

What You Do:

1. Trace and cut out all templates from the card stock, as pictured (A).

2. On the wrong side of the large yellow piece of card stock, with the red marker, write the message *Hot dog! We're having a party!*

3. List other party details below: where, when, time, RSVP, etc.

4. To put the invite together, start by gluing the small yellow piece to the front of the dog, ¾ inch (1.9 cm) down from the top of the dog's back (B).

5. Next glue the yellow piece with the message to the back of the dog, making sure that the bottom of both yellow pieces are perfectly lined up. There should be approximately ½ inch (1.3 cm) of yellow paper visible above the top of the dog's back (C).

6. Finish by folding the indicated area on the ear. Attach to the dog's head using the glue stick, and then glue the glittery paper to the dog's back (D).

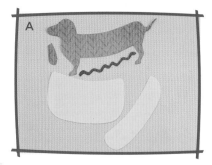

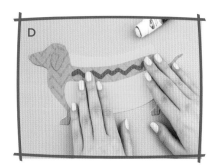

Bulldog Bunting

Don't miss the op-paw-tunity to add extra decorative touches to your dog-themed party!

What You Need:

Pencil

Templates (page 103)

Card stock, 24 × 24 inches (61 × 61 cm) in turquoise; 12 × 12 inches (30.5 × 30.5 cm) in yellow; 12 × 12 inches (30.5 × 30.5 cm) in white; 8½ × 11 inches (21.6 × 27.9 cm) in hot pink

Scissors

Glue stick

10 rhinestones, ½ inch (1.3 cm) in black

50 silver stars, ¼ inch (6 mm)

8 tassel garlands in pink

Yarn, 6 feet (1.8 m) in white

Masking tape

What You Do:

1. Trace the templates so that you have the following pieces: 3 turquoise heads, 6 turquoise ears, 2 yellow heads, 4 yellow ears, 10 pink inner ears, 10 pink noses, 10 white muzzles **(A)**. Cut them out.

2. For each dog's head, start by gluing the inner ears to the outer ears, then the ear to the head **(B)**.

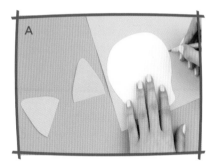 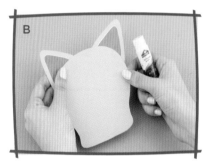

3. Next glue on the muzzle and the nose, followed by adding 2 rhinestone eyes and 5 stars to each side of the dog's muzzle.

4. Glue eyes and stars to muzzle **(C, D)**.

5. Fold the back template on the indicated marks, then add glue to the folds at the top and the bottoms **(E)**.

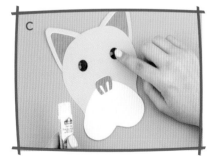  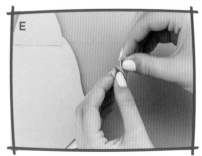

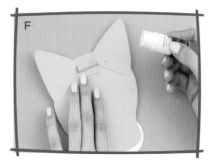

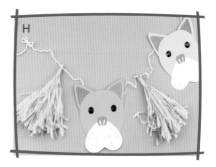

Note: Please allow the glue at least thirty minutes of drying time before hanging.

6. Stick this to the back of the dog's head, in between the ears **(F)**. Let dry for a few minutes.

7. To assemble the bunting, string a tassel garland 8 inches (20.3 cm) from the left side of the yarn, then add one blue dog **(G)**.

8. Continue adding dogs in alternating colors with one tassel garland in between until you have added the last tassel garland **(H)**.

9. Space as you like, then add a piece of masking tape to either side of each back tab.

10. Hang and enjoy!

Paw-ty Favors

Let your guests know they made an impression with these sweet party favors!
Just remember that drying times with air-dry clay can vary, so be sure to
start this project well in advance of your party date.

What You Need:

Newspaper

Rolling pin

Air-dry clay, 2-pound (.91 kg) container

Heart-shaped cookie cutter (approximately 1½ × 2 inches in diameter)

Chopstick

Permanent marker

Chrome spray paint

Decoupage medium in shiny finish

Ribbon, cord, raffia, or other material for hanging, 10 inches (25.4 cm) in length and ¼ inch (6 mm) in width, 1 piece for each party favor

What You Do:

1. Cover your work surface with newspaper to protect it from the spray paint.

2. With the rolling pin, roll out the clay to a thickness of ¼ inch (6 mm) **(A)**.

3. Use the cookie cutter to make a heart cutout for each one of your guests **(B)**.

4. Remove the excess clay from around all of the hearts.

5. Use the chopstick to make two holes through each side of the heart, as pictured **(C)**.

6. Use the end of a permanent marker to make the large circular impression toward the bottom center of the heart **(D)**.

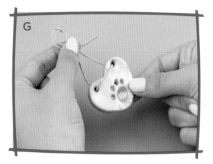

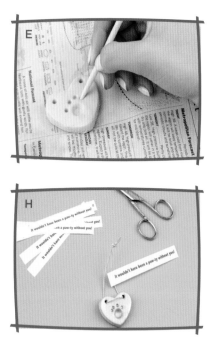

Optional: Print the message
It wouldn't have been a
paw-ty without you! *on*
a sheet of paper, repeating
for as many guests as are
attending. Cut the messages
into strips and attach to the
ribbon **(H)**.

7. In an arc around the top of the circle impression, gently press the clay using the chopstick to make the paw pads **(E)**.

8. Allow plenty of time to dry. (Follow the manufacturer's instructions, as drying times vary.)

9. When the clay has dried completely, take the hearts outside and spray with chrome spray paint **(F)**. Spray the top side with an even, sweeping motion, and then, after it dries, flip over to spray the back. When you're finished, none of the white clay should be visible.

10. Paint the top with a shiny decoupage medium, allowing at least 25 minutes to dry. After it dries, flip over to paint the backside, and again allow at least 25 minutes to dry.

11. Starting from the backside, string the ribbon through both holes, as pictured **(G)**, and tie the two ends together in an overhand knot ½ inch away from the top.

Bone Appétit Place Cards

Made to match the Bulldog Bunting (page 57), these place cards couldn't be easier to put together, and they add an extra-special touch to your guests' place settings.

What You Need (per place card):

Pencil

Template (page 104)

White card stock, 5½ × 2½ inches (14 × 6.4 cm) per card

Scissors

Marker

Glue stick

3 silver stars, ¼ inch (6 mm)

What You Do:

1. Trace the template on the wrong side of the white card stock paper (A).

2. Cleanly cut out the shape on the traced line (B).

3. Flip the card right-side up, then, with marker, write your guest's name across the bone (C).

4. Finish by gluing 2 or 3 silver stars onto the top-left corner (D).

5. Repeat steps 1 through 4 until you have a place card for each of your guests.

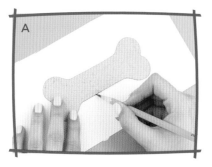

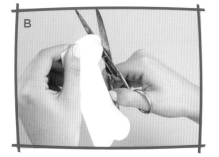

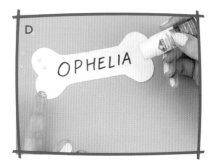

Paw Print Party Plates

Great parties are made in the details! This sweet and easy project is just what you need to add a little something extra to your dog-themed soirée.

What You Need:

Round paper confetti,
½ × ½ inch (1.3 × 1.3 cm)
in yellow

Paper hole punch, ¼ inch
(6 mm)

Square paper plates,
one for each guest,
10¼ × 10¼ inches
(26 × 26 cm) in aqua
(or color of your choice)

Glue stick, nontoxic

What You Do (for each plate):

1. Place a stack of the confetti pieces into the hole punch and squeeze to punch out **(A)**. (The little pieces that come out will be used for creating the paw print shape, so you will need four of these small circles for every piece of confetti glued to the plate.)

2. Start gluing pieces of the full-size confetti around the edge of the plate, as pictured **(B)**.

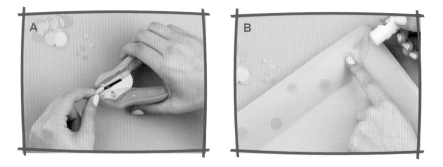

3. Glue four of the little circles that you created with the hole punch around the top of each piece of confetti in an arc **(C)**.

4. Repeat step 3 until all of the confetti look like paw prints **(D)**.

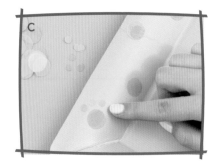
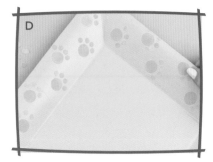

Star-Spaniel'd Tablecloth

This hand-printed, stamped tablecloth makes a fetching addition to your table décor.

What You Need (per place card):

Pencil

Templates (page 104)

Scissors

Adhesive foam, one sheet measuring at least 3 × 6 inches (7.6 × 15.2 cm)

Cardboard, 2 squares, one 3¼ × 3¼ (8.2 × 8.2 cm) and one 1½ × 1½ inches (3.8 × 3.8 cm)

Fabric paint in pink and yellow

2 paper plates

Scrap paper or fabric (optional)

Tablecloth, 3.5 × 3.5 feet (1.1 × 1.1 m)

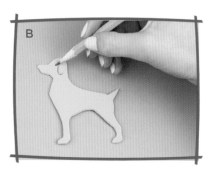

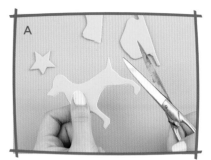

What You Do:

1. Trace the templates onto each of the foam pieces and cut out **(A)**.

2. With a sharpened pencil, press down firmly on the dog-shaped foam to indent the area at the dog's eye and ear, as indicated on the template **(B)**.

3. Adhere the foam pieces to the pieces of cardboard **(C)**. These will be your stamps.

4. Squeeze some pink paint onto one of the paper plates.

5. Press dog stamp foam-side down on the plate until the foam is covered in a thin, even layer of paint.

   Tip: Although this is an easy project, it can still be helpful to practice printing with the stamps before making marks on your table cloth. You may do so either with a scrap piece of paper or fabric.

6. Place the dog stamp facedown onto the tablecloth, applying even pressure **(D)**.

7. Repeat steps 5 and 6 until you are happy with the coverage of dogs on your tablecloth.

8. Clean your dog stamp by repeatedly pressing it onto the scrap paper until it is no longer printing.

9. Squeeze some yellow paint onto the other paper plate.

10. Repeat steps 5 through 7 with the star stamp **(E)**.

11. Clean the stamp by repeatedly pressing onto the scrap paper until it is no longer printing.

12. Allow the tablecloth to dry flat for at least 4 hours before using. Allow at least 72 hours before washing.

For Your Dog

It's a dog's life, so they say, and with these cleverly crafted
projects, your dog's life just got a whole lot better!

"Rub My Belly" Bandana

If your dog is anything like mine, she is never willing to pass over a good belly rub.
This humorous bandana project just says what she was already thinking!

What You Need:

Erasable fabric pen

Template (page 104)

Bandana, 21 × 21 inches
(53.4 × 53.4 cm)

Embroidery needle

Embroidery thread, black

Scissors

What You Do:

1. Transfer the template design onto one of the corners of the bandana with an erasable fabric pen **(A, B)**.

 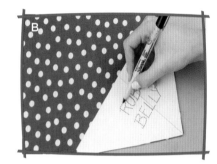

2. Stitch over all of the letters in black thread with a Chain Stitch (page ix) **(C, D)**.

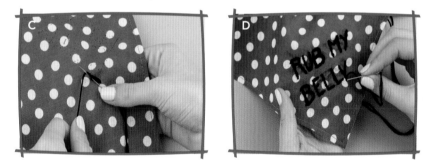

3. Fold the bandana in half, then roll down until it is the right length for your dog's chest.

4. Tie around your dog's neck with an overhand knot, but not too tight! Your dog should be comfortable.

Adjustable Collar

Making your own dog's collar gives you ultimate control! Pick the color, width, and even the perfect closure. You're certain to be a hit at the dog park with this project. Nylon webbing and closures can be found in both craft and hardware stores.

What You Need:

Cloth tape measure

Nylon webbing, 1 inch (2.5 cm) wide × the circumference of your dog's neck plus 10 inches (25.4 cm) in yellow

Lighter

Tri-glide, 1 inch (2.5 cm) width in silver finish

Sewing machine

Sewing thread, yellow

Buckle, 1 inch (2.5 cm) width in silver finish

D-ring, 1 inch (2.5 cm) width in silver finish

What You Do:

1. Measure your dog's neck.

2. Cut a piece of webbing at this measurement, plus 10 inches (25.4 cm).

3. Use the lighter to gently fuse the cut ends of the nylon webbing (A). This will prevent fraying.

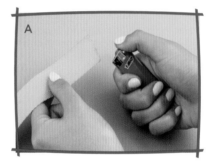 

4. Insert the tri-glide onto the webbing (B).

5. Fold back 2 inches (5.1 cm) and sew down on the sewing machine (C), with two side-by-side rows of stitches.

6. On the other side of the webbing, insert the male side of the buckle (D).

7. Slide the loose end through the tri-glide (E).

  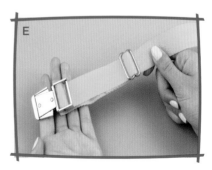

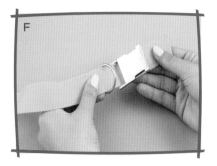
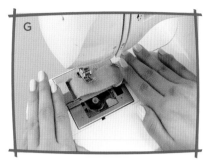
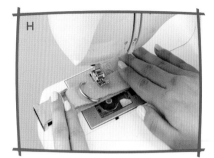

8. Slide the D-ring onto the open side of the webbing and the female buckle (F).

9. Fold the webbing so that there is an overlap of 2 inches (5.1 cm), then stitch two rows of stitches in front of the buckle (G).

10. Slide the D-ring up to that row of stitches, and then sew two more rows of stitches behind it (H).

Leather-Trimmed Leash

Handcrafted leashes are quite costly. This project lets you create your own well-made leash that's not only beautiful but also super affordable. The best place to find the rope and closures needed for this project is your local hardware or farm-supply store.

What You Need:

Tape measure

Rope, 7 feet (2.1 m) in length, approximately 1½ inch (3.8 cm) in diameter in white

Scissors

Sewing needle

Nylon sewing thread in white

Vinyl or leather, 2 pieces, each 3 × 3 inches (7.6 × 7.6 cm)

Snap hook in silver finish

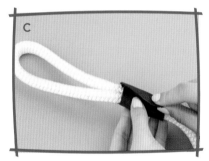

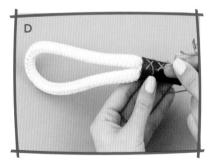

Tip: You may want to shorten or lengthen the length of the rope used based on the size of your dog.

What You Do:

1. Measure 7 feet (2.1 m) of rope and cut.

2. Create a fold 8 inches (20.3 cm) away from one end (A).

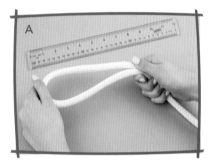

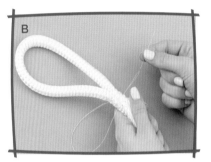

3. Use the needle and nylon thread to sew the loose end to the rope as shown (B). (You may want to fray the very end somewhat to help it lay flat.)

4. Alternate sewing through the two layers with wrapping the thread around the pieces to strengthen.

5. Wrap the vinyl or leather around the rope where the pieces are sewn together (C).

6. Stitch the overlapped pieces together with a Criss-Cross Stitch as pictured (D).

7. Slip the trigger snap 3 inches (7.6 cm) onto the other end of the rope and fold (E).

8. Secure the two pieces of rope by repeating steps 3 through 6.

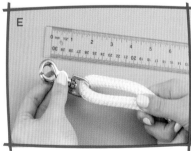

Doggie Bag Holder

Picking up poop is a part of life when you have a dog. If it's possible to do this daily chore in style, then this is the way to do it.

What You Need:

Erasable fabric pen, pencil, or chalk

Templates (page 105)

Scissors

Faux leather or leather, 8 × 3 inches (20.3 × 7.6 cm) in tan, 4 × 3 inches (10.2 × 7.6 cm) in yellow

Awl

Embroidery thread, 1 skein in yellow

Embroidery needle

Snap clip in silver finish

Transfer tape

Hand-sewing punch

Hand punch, ⅛ inch (3 mm) circle

Collar button, ¼ inch (6 mm) in silver finish

Pre-rolled dog waste bags

What You Do:

1. Trace all templates onto the materials and cut out with scissors. Use the awl to make all indicated holes on the template for sewing (A).

2. Attach the bottom of the tab piece of faux leather with a Double Running Stitch (page ix) (B).

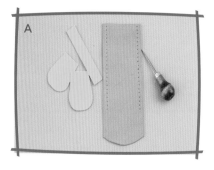 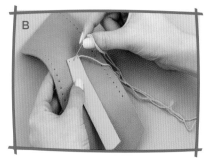

3. Slide the snap clip over the other end of the strip before stitching it down with a Double Running Stitch and Criss Cross Stitch (page ix), as pictured (C).

4. Add transfer tape to the long sides on the back of the material (D).

5. Remove the paper backing and stick the side pieces into place (E).

6. Align the hand-sewing punch with the marks made from the awl and squeeze to make holes through both pieces.

 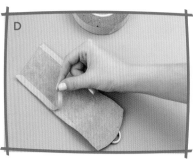 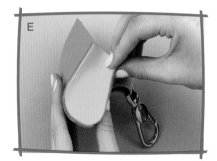

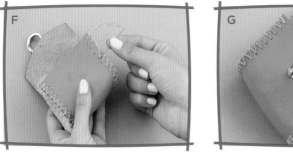

7. Stitch both sides together with a Double Whip Stitch **(F)**.

8. Use the hand punch to make the 2 round holes, as indicated by the template, and add the collar button to the hole in the front **(G)**.

9. Place the bags in the container **(H)** and clip to your leash.

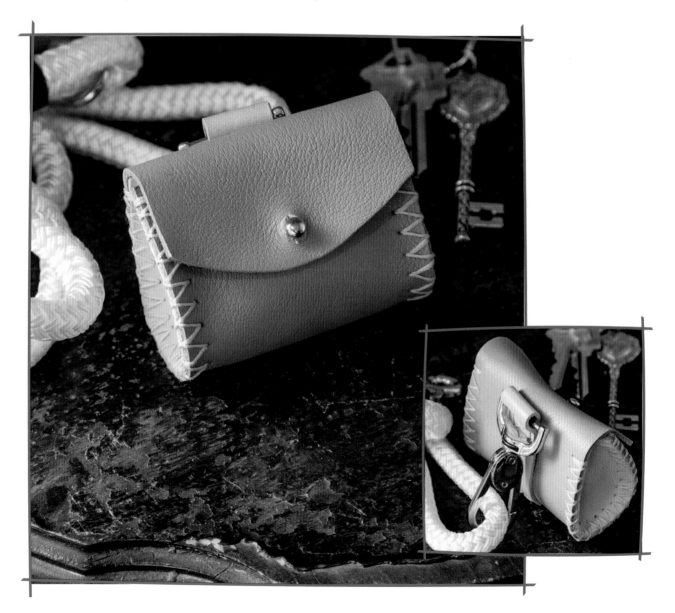

Sharker's Sweater

If it's cold outside enough for you to need a sweater, then your dog probably needs one, too! This is a great opportunity to upcycle an old sweater; measure carefully to make sure you have enough of each.

What You Need:

Template (page 106)

Printed velour, large enough to fit your dog

Cotton batting, large enough to fit your dog

Knitted fabric, large enough to fit your dog

Pins

Sewing machine

Sewing needle

Sewing thread in a color complementary to your chosen fabrics

Hook-and-loop tape

What You Do:

1. Because this project is customized to the size of your dog, start by taking three measurements:

   • Measure your dog from its lower neck to the place on its back that lines up with its back legs.

   • Take a measurement of the girth, starting at the top of the back around the belly and back.

   • Measure the circumference of the base of the neck.

2. Enlarge the templates to match the measurements you've taken. This will ensure that the pattern is the right size. Remember that this template has sewing allowance included, so the final product will be a ½ inch (1.3 cm) smaller all around. Also customize the strap lengths as needed.

3. Lay the adjusted template onto each of the three materials, trace, and cut out (A).

4. Stack the three pieces together in the following order (B):

   • **velour:** right-side up

   • **knit fabric:** right-side down

   • **cotton batting:** on top

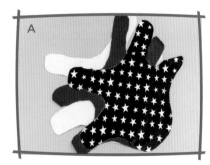
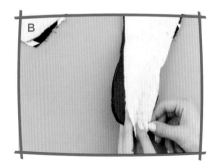

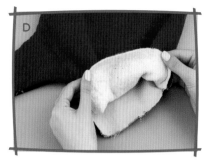

5. Pin all around.

6. Place on the sewing machine and stitch with ½ inch (1.3 cm) sewing allowance from the bottom all the way around **(C)**. When you get back to the bottom, leave a 4-inch (10.2 cm) opening.

7. Remove the pins and use the opening to turn right side out **(D)**.

8. Fold the raw edges at the opening inward and use the needle and thread to stitch closed with a Double Running Stitch (page ix) **(E)**.

9. Finish by stitching hook-and-loop tape onto all four of the straps, as shown in photo **(F)**.

Upcycled Dog Toy

Aside from providing your dog with hours of fun, this project is also a great way to upcycle a few of your old T-shirts.

What You Need:

Scissors

3 T-shirts in gray, pink, and yellow or the colors of your choice

2 rubber bands

Sewing needle

Sewing thread

What You Do:

1. Cut the hem off the bottom of the shirts. Then, from the bottom of each of the three shirts, cut two horizontal strips of fabric, each 2 inches wide (5.1 cm) **(A)**.

2. Connect the six strips by binding them with a rubber band ½ inch from their top edge, then arrange by color as seen in the photo **(B)**.

3. Braid them together as shown **(C)**.

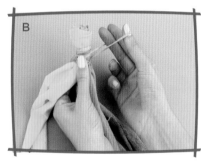

4. When your braid is approximately 12 inches (30.5 cm) long, bind the bottom of the braid with your second rubber band **(D)**.

5. Trim the excess material below the rubber band to ½ inch (1.3 cm).

6. Form the braid into a circle, with the two rubber bands overlapped **(E)**.

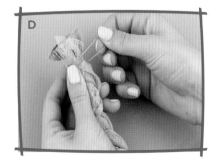

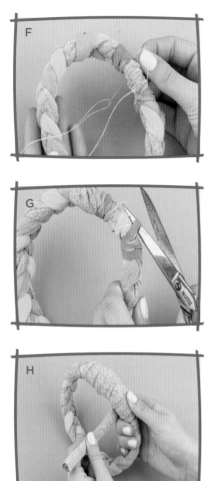

7. Take your needle and thread and sew through all six strips of fabric at the overlap **(F)**.

8. For strength, alternate sewing through the strips with wrapping the thread around them all.

9. Repeat steps 7 and 8 until you are sure that all of the strips are bound together, and then use your scissors to cut away the rubber bands **(G)**.

10. Cut one more strip from a shirt, measuring 2 × 10 inches (5.1 × 25.4 cm).

11. Sew one of the 2-inch (5.1 cm) ends to the area where all six strips are joined.

12. Tightly wrap the remaining length of the strip around the sewn strips until the thread is not visible **(H)**.

13. Finish by discreetly sewing the loose end of the strap down.

Cozy Dog Bed

This soft and comfy dog bed lets your mutt lounge in style.

What You Need:

Erasable fabric pen, pencil, or chalk

Template (page 107)

Faux fleece fabric, 24 × 18 inches (61 × 45.7 cm) in beige

Midweight to heavyweight fabric, 24 × 18 inches (61 × 45.7 cm) in beige or another solid color

Scissors

Midweight to heavyweight fabric, 5 × 70 inches (12.7 × 177.8 cm) in pattern of your choice

Pins

Sewing machine

Polyester filling

Sewing needle

Sewing thread, beige or complementary solid color

What You Do:

1. Trace the template onto the faux fleece and onto the beige fabric. Cut them both out.

2. Cut the patterned fabric into a rectangle measuring 5 × 70 inches (12.7 × 177.8 cm).

3. Pin one of the long edges of the patterned fabric all around the faux fleece, with right sides together **(A)**.

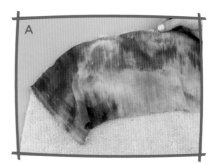

4. Fold the overlapping edges of the short end back, away from the right side of the fabric, and pin.

5. Stitch this short edge closed on the sewing machine.

6. Stitch all around on the faux fleece fabric, ½ inch (1.3 cm) away from the edge **(B)**. Remove all of the pins.

7. Now pin the beige fabric to the remaining long edge of the patterned fabric with right sides together.

8. Stitch all around on the beige fabric, ½ inch (1.3 cm) away from the edge, leaving a 4-inch (10.2 cm) opening. Remove all the pins.

9. Flip right-side out and stuff with the polyester filling **(C)**. You want the bed to be full but not overstuffed.

10. Finish the bed by folding back the fabric at the 4-inch opening (10.2 cm), so that no raw edges are showing and sewing closed with a Double Running Stitch **(D)**.

Note: *This template is for a dog bed measuring 22 × 16 inches (55.9 × 40.6 cm). Reduce or enlarge, as needed, to accommodate the size of your dog.*

Stamped Name Tags

Forget waiting weeks to order a custom tag for your dog. Make one yourself using a metal-stamping kit, purchased from your local craft store. You can include all the vital stats, like your address and phone number, just in case your furry friend ever gets lost.

What You Need:

Ruler

Metal tag (bone-shaped or any shape you choose), 1¾ × ¾ inches (4.4 × 1.9 cm)

Permanent marker in black

Stamping plate

Metal alphabet stamps

Copper-headed mallet

Soft cloth

Jump ring, ¼ inch (6 mm)

Ear plugs (optional)

What You Do:

Tip: You may need ear plugs, as the hammering you'll need to do for this project can be a bit loud.

1. Use the ruler to find the mark just slightly lower than the center on the tag, and with the permanent marker, draw a horizontal line across the tag **(A)**. This will be used for keeping your letters straight.

2. Place the tag on the stamping plate. Place the middle letter in your dog's name at the center point of the tag, just above the line. If your dog has an even number of letters in its name, place just to the side of the center. Starting at the middle will ensure that the dog's name is centered on the tag.

3. Double-check that your letter is straight and facing the correct direction, then, using the mallet, firmly strike the top of the stamp **(B)**.

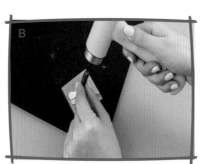
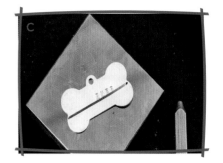

4. Line up the next letter in the dog's name, directly next to the letter you just made, and strike with mallet.

5. Repeat step 4, working from left to right, until you have reached the last letter in the dog's name **(C)**.

6. Add the letters at the beginning of the dog's name by adding them one by one in reverse order, from right to left **(D)**.

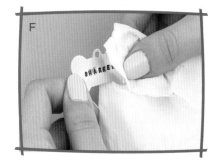

7. When you have finished stamping, mark over all of the letters with the permanent marker **(E)**. Be sure to get into the grooves of every letter, as this will help the name stand out.

8. Wipe with the soft cloth until all of the marker has been wiped away from everywhere except inside the letters **(F)**.

9. Add to your dog's collar with a jump ring.

Painted Dog Bowl

Add some flair to your dog's bowl with this very colorful and surprisingly easy-to-do project. No painting experience required.

What You Need:

Nontoxic acrylic crafting paint in pink, yellow, blue, and black

Flat paintbrush, 1 inch (2.5 cm) wide

Porcelain dog bowl

What You Do:

1. Start with the pink paint, make 1½-inch-wide (3.8 cm) strokes on the bowl. Space them out, and be sure to vary the direction of the strokes.

   Tip: Be sure to clean your paintbrush before switching colors to prevent colors from becoming muddled.

2. Repeat step 1, but this time with the yellow paint, and then with the blue. Allow time for the paint to dry.

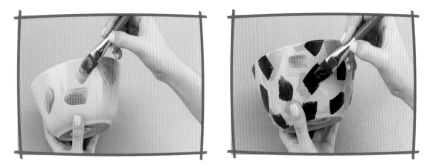

3. To finish, paint strokes with the black paint. It's okay for the black to overlap some of the other colors. This will help to tie the design together in a finished look.

4. Allow plenty of time to dry before use, and clean as needed with a soft sponge.

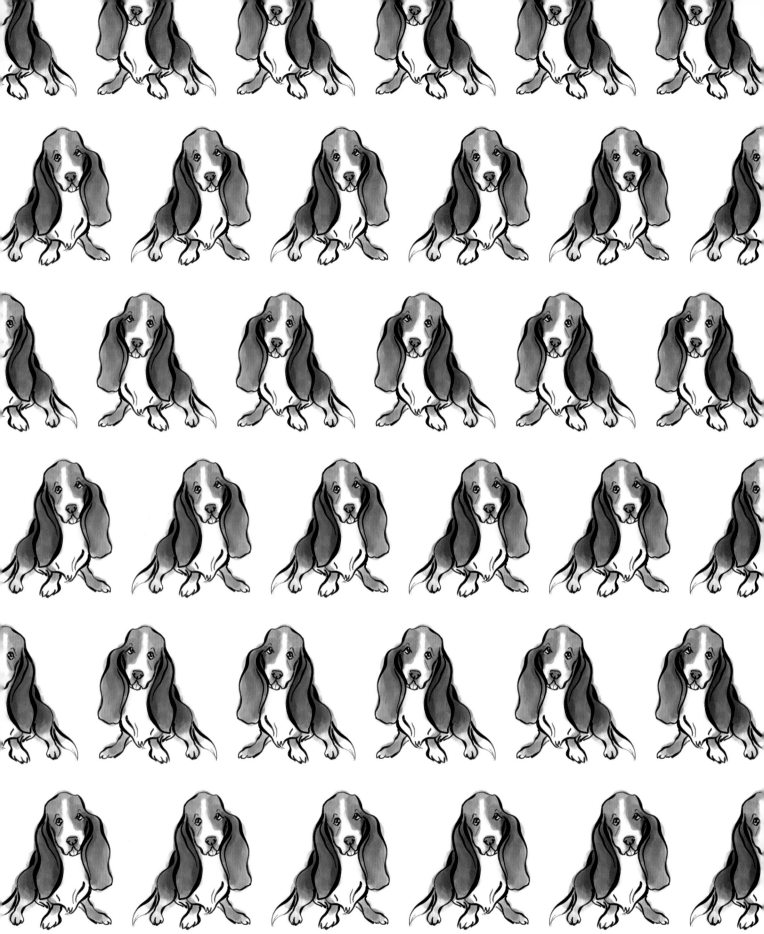

Templates

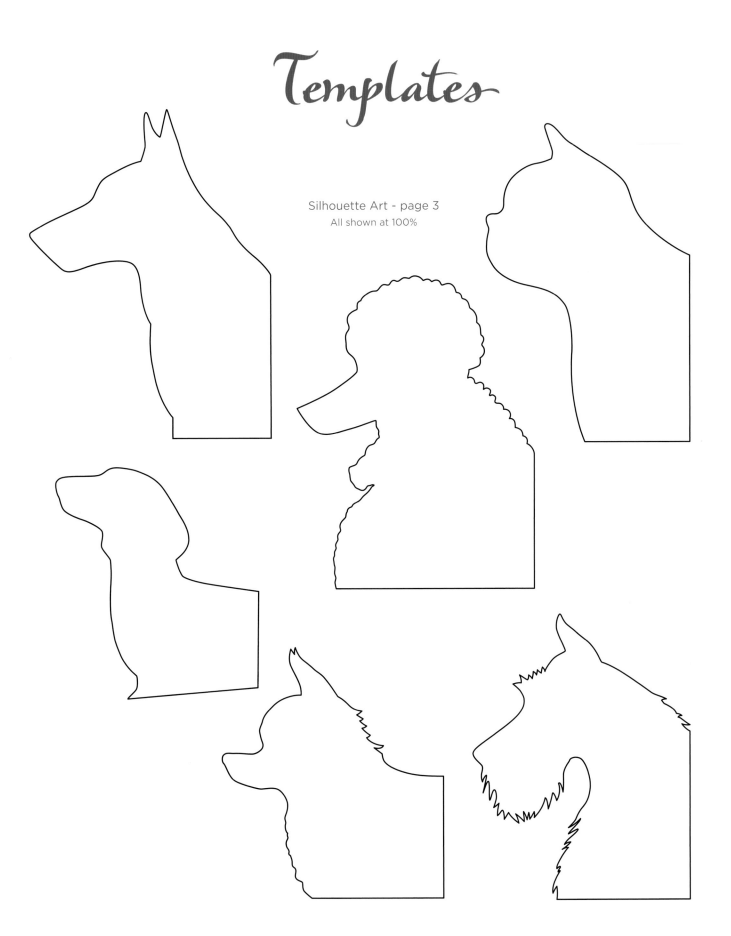

Silhouette Art - page 3
All shown at 100%

Bone-Shaped Welcome Mat - page 11
Enlarge by 335%

Paw Prints Rolling Pin Stamp - page 7
Shown at 100%

ALL YOU NEED IS LOVE… & DOGS

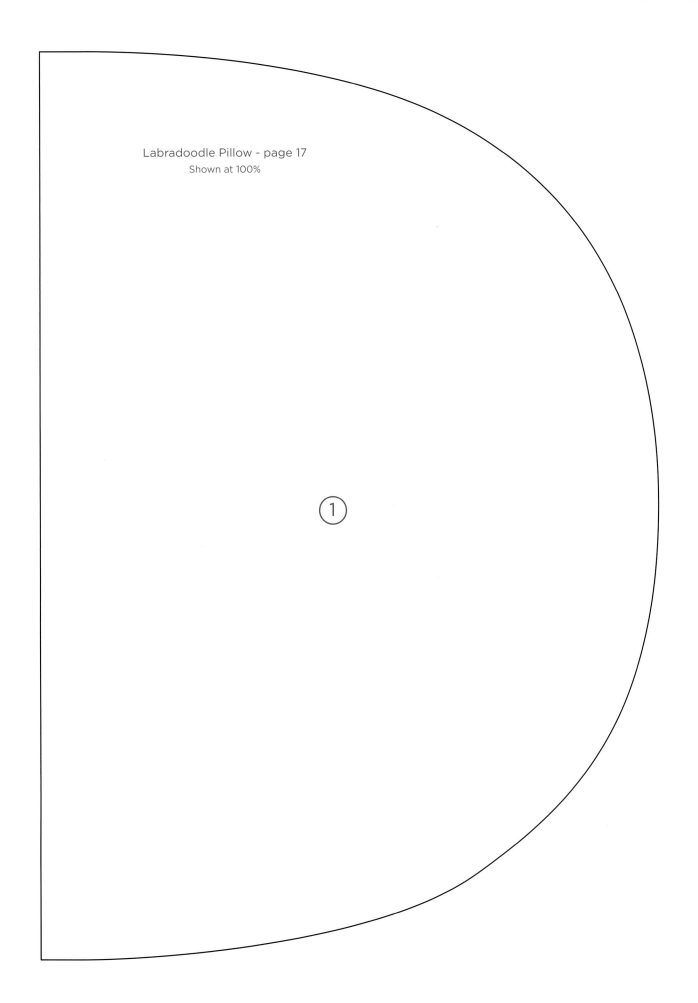

Labradoodle Pillow - page 17
Shown at 100%

1

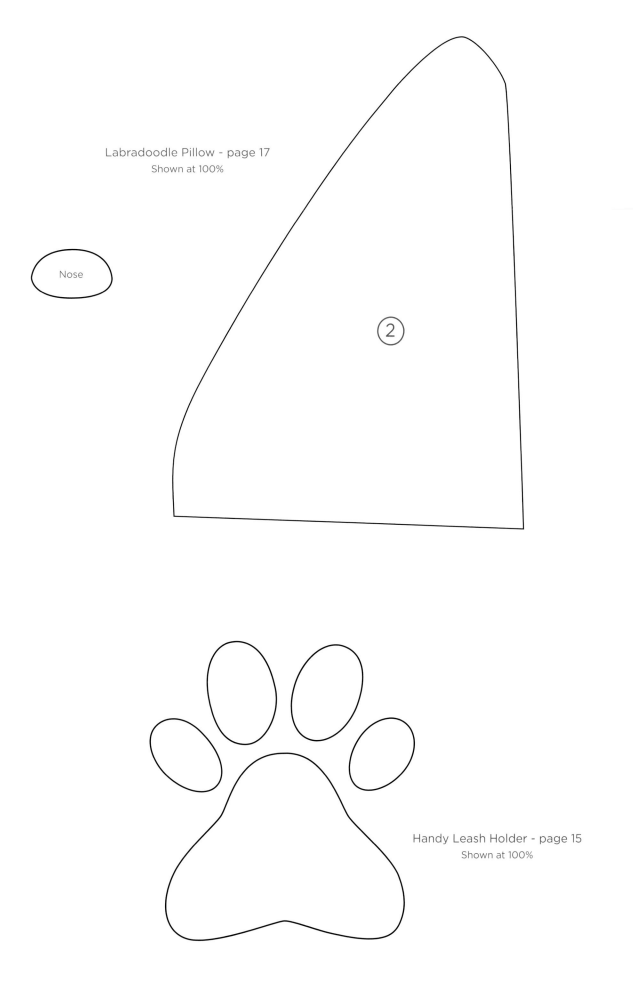

Labradoodle Pillow - page 17
Shown at 100%

Nose

2

Handy Leash Holder - page 15
Shown at 100%

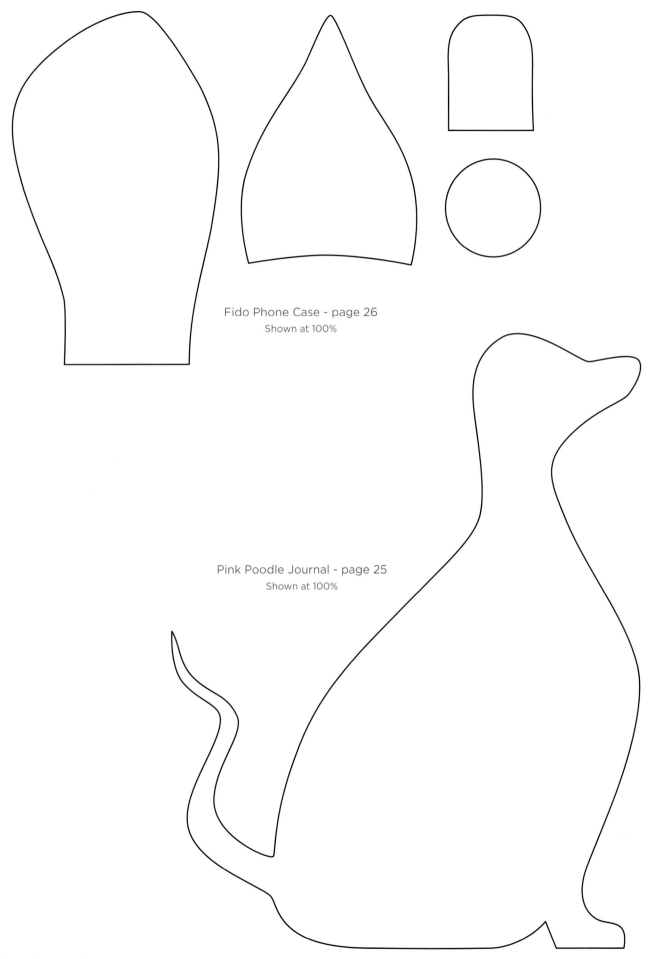

Fido Phone Case - page 26
Shown at 100%

Pink Poodle Journal - page 25
Shown at 100%

Dachshund Shopping Tote - page 31
Shown at 100%

Lotsa Spots Jeans - page 42
Shown at 100%

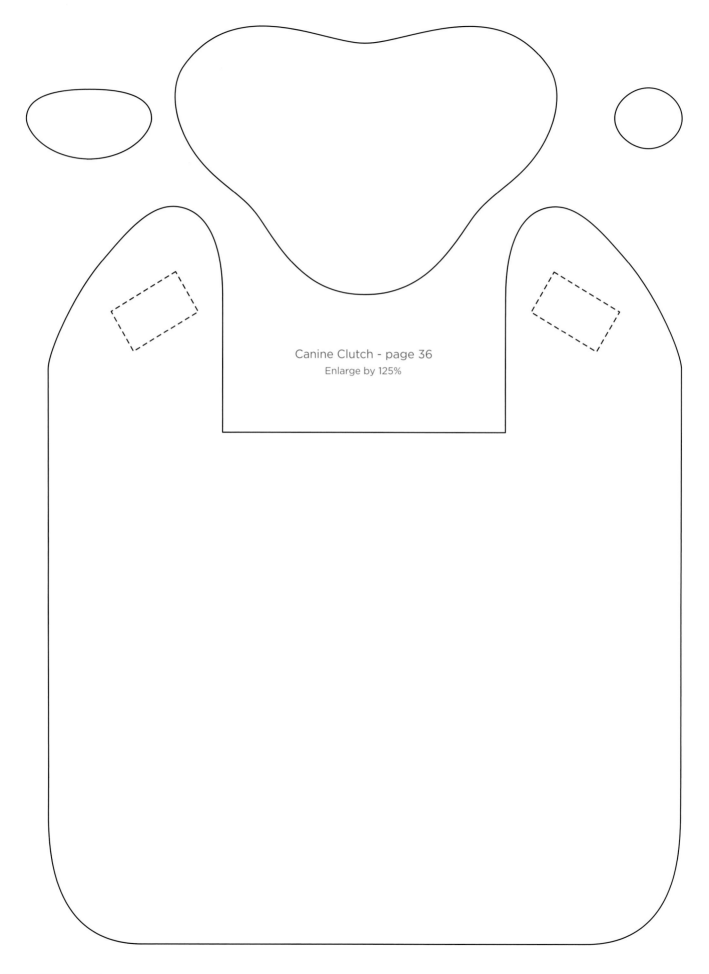

Canine Clutch - page 36
Enlarge by 125%

Embroidered Dog Patches - page 44
Shown at 100%

Paw Print Elbow Patches - page 46
Shown at 100%

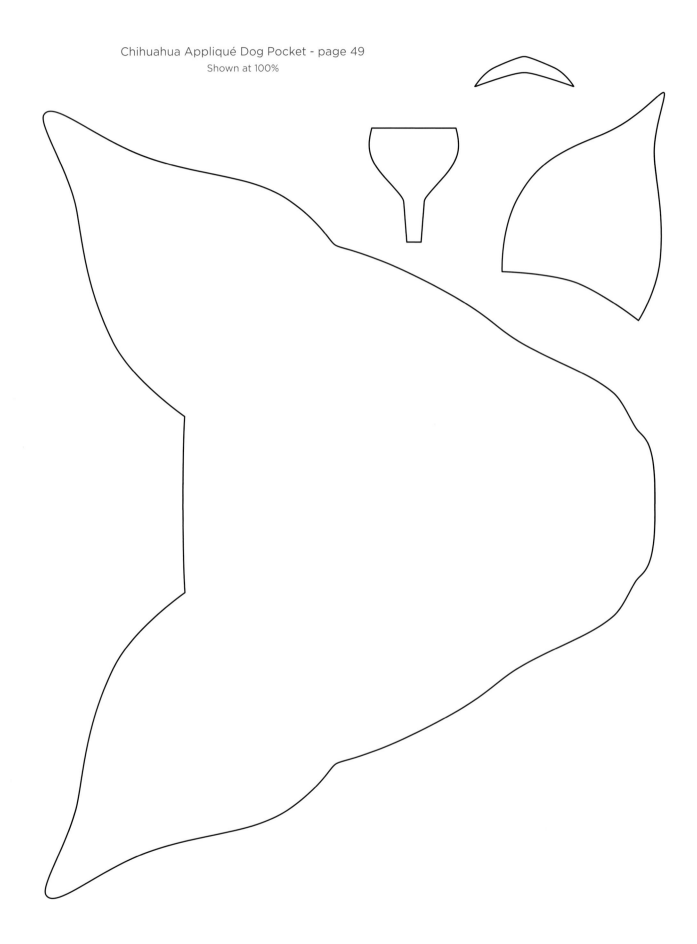

Painted Pups Stenciled Shirt- page 50
Enlarge by 125%

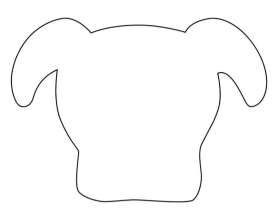

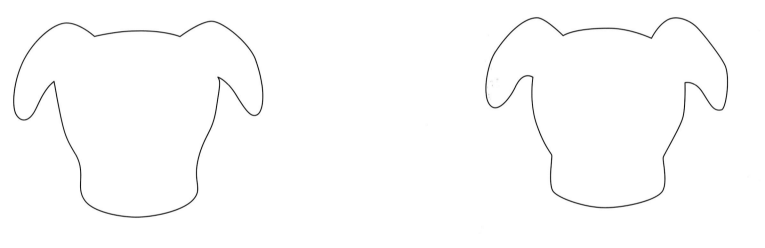

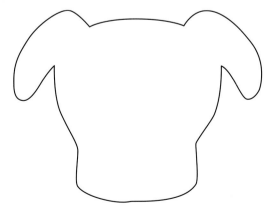

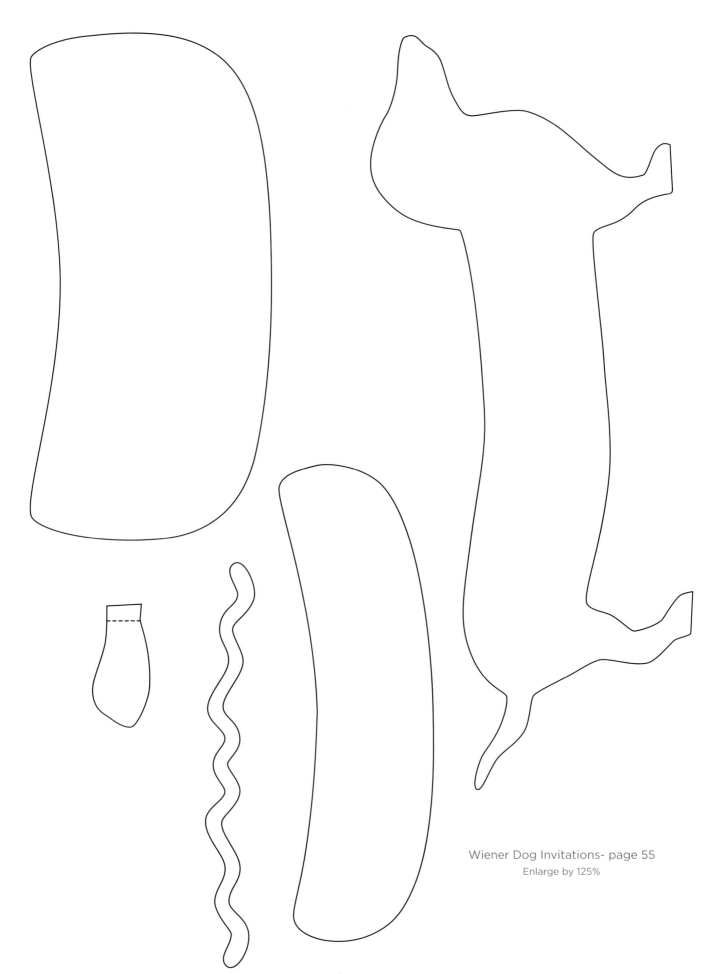

Wiener Dog Invitations- page 55
Enlarge by 125%

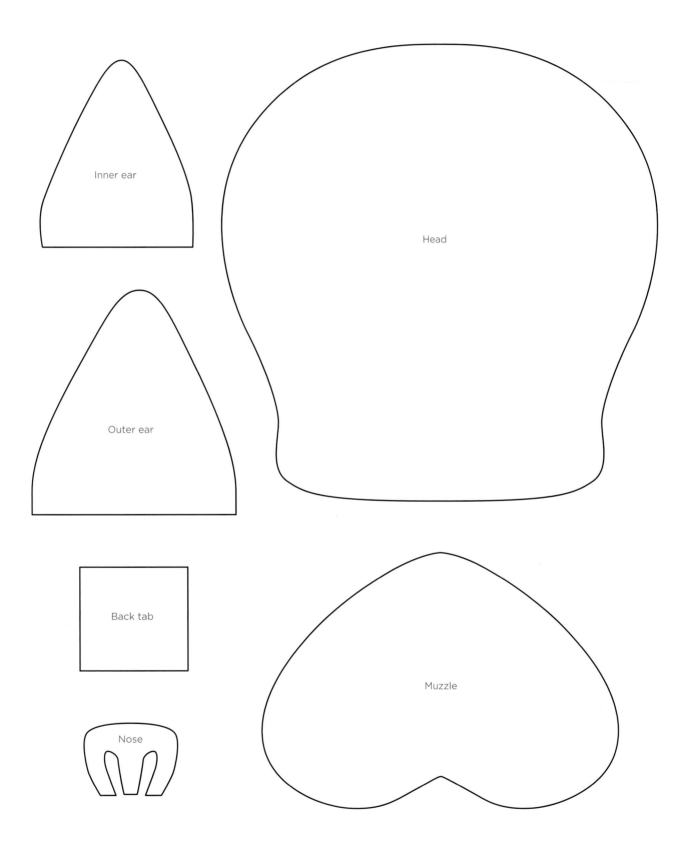

Inner ear

Head

Outer ear

Back tab

Muzzle

Nose

Bone Appétit Place Cards - page 63
Shown at 100%

"Rub My Belly" Bandana - page 71
Shown at 100%

Star-Spaniel'd Tablecloth - page 66
Shown at 100%

RUB MY
BELLY

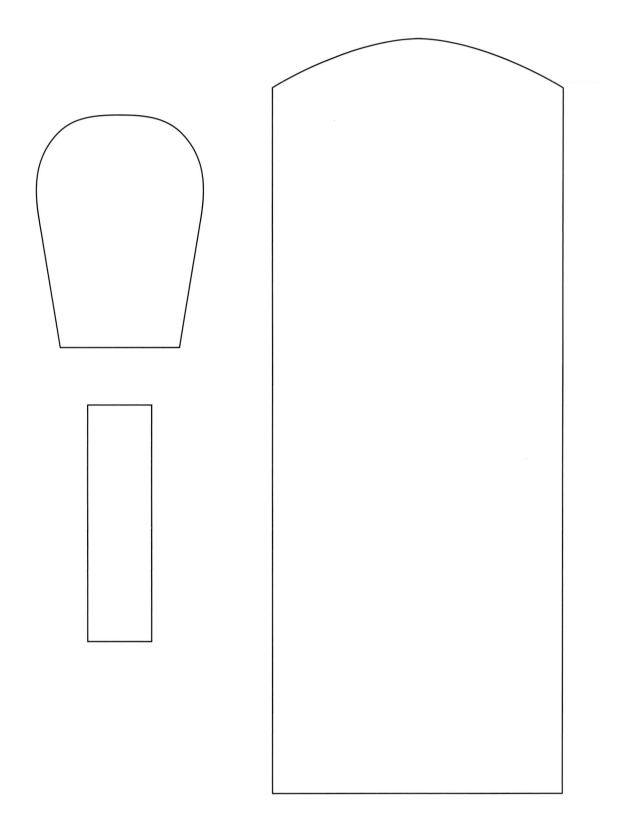

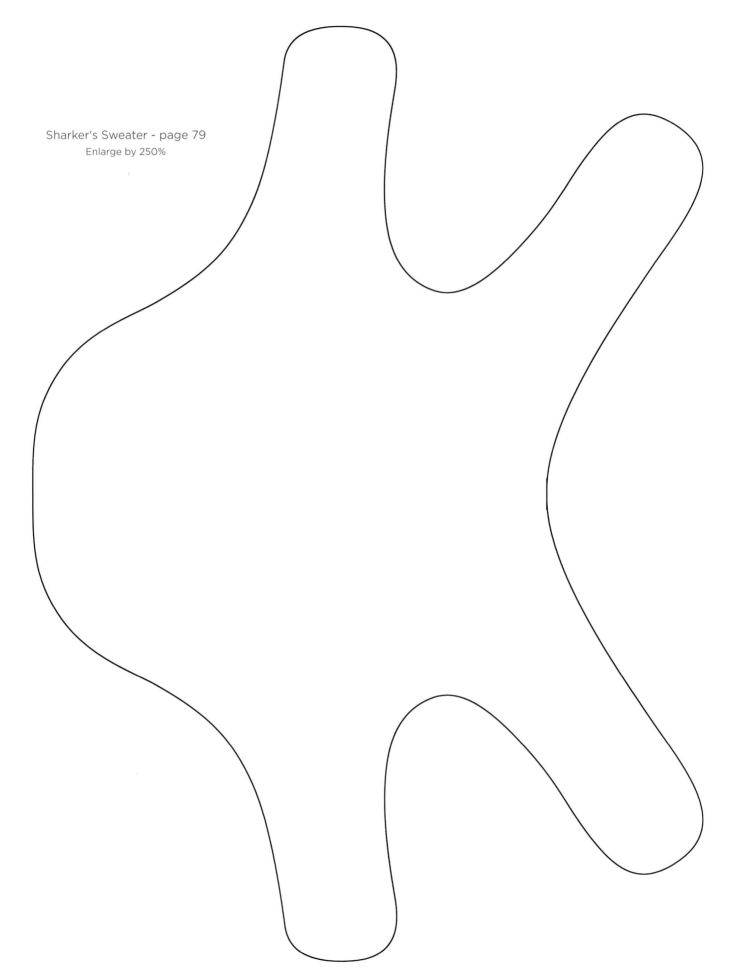

Sharker's Sweater - page 79
Enlarge by 250%

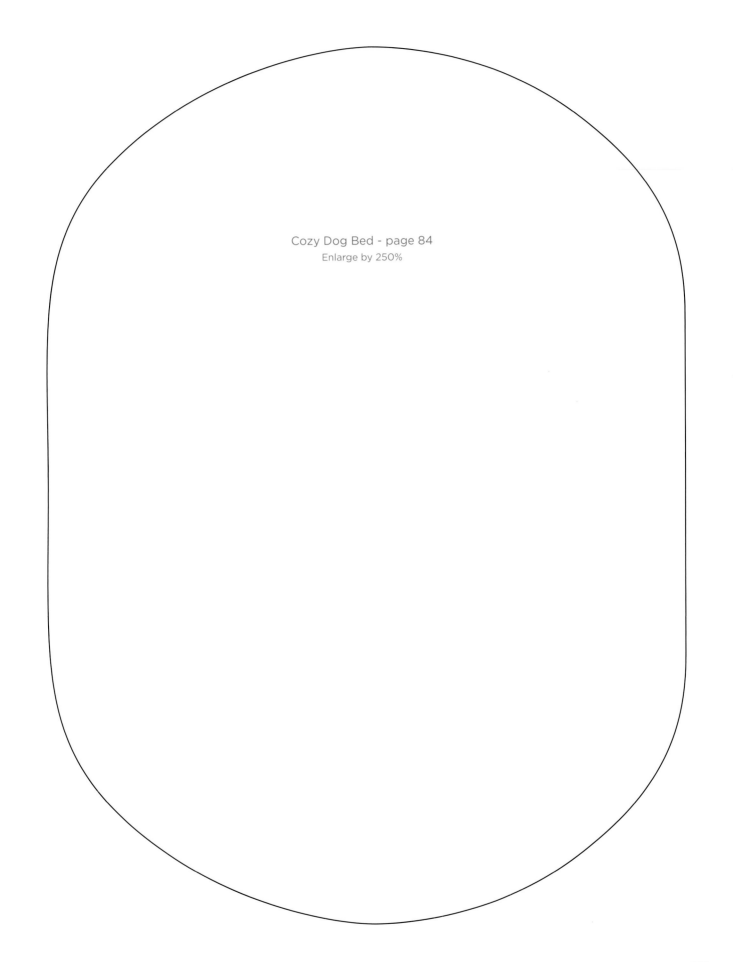

Cozy Dog Bed - page 84
Enlarge by 250%

About the Author

Kat Roberts is an artist and fashion teacher living in Brooklyn, New York. In addition to this book, she has authored a number of other crafting books, including her most recent, *Crafting for Cat Ladies*.

Acknowledgments

I have so many people to thank for helping this book come into being!

My gratitude goes out my terrific agent Kate McKean. The wonderful team at Lark: my editor Wendy Williams and the creative team, Chris Bain, Shannon Plunkett, Kayla Overbey, Lorie Pagnozzi, Elizabeth Mihaltse Lindy, Susan Levitt, and Jo Obarowski. And thank you always to my ever-patient and loving family, Ophelia, Fiffe, and, of course, my mom, Katy.

Finally, I would be remiss not to take a moment to acknowledge the primary inspiration for this book: my number-one bad bitch, Sharker. Before we adopted her, my family had a lot of very specific notions about what the perfect dog for us would be—the breed, the age, the personality, etc. Then came Sharker. She met exactly zero of our criteria, but there was no denying that she was the one for us. To be quite honest, she seemed like she *really* needed a family to take her home and love her. And so we did. She has taught our family so much about patience and kindness and made our hearts grow a whole lot bigger. She is, by far, the strangest creature I've ever met, and we wouldn't have it any other way. So thank you, Sharker! Thank you for constantly surprising us and for always keeping our family laughing. We love you beyond words! And thank you also to Badass Brooklyn Animal Rescue for bringing this bizarre beauty into our lives.

About the Dogs

No dogs were harmed in the making of this book!

Daisy is a three-year-old Australian cattle dog/terrier mix whom Wendy Williams and her family adopted from a shelter in Long Island, New York. While she didn't bark for the first three months in her new home, she did manage to eat four pairs of shoes and all the apples from a backyard tree. She has since grown out of both of those habits and is happy at home in Brooklyn, laying by the radiator or on the nearest person's foot.

Leela is a three-year old Maltipoo rescue from California, adopted from Pasadena Humane Society & SPCA, by Jo Obarowski's family. She likes sniffing telephone poles on her daily walks, licking her brothers' Lex and Mason's faces and feet, and waiting for dad Steve to share his dinner with her, even at the table. Another favorite pastime is getting up close and personal to the family's bearded dragon, Zilla. Leela's mama (Jo) is super excited about this book!

Ruban was named after the island he was found and rescued on—the small island of Aruba. He was found in June 2017 by the local rescue agency Sgt. Pepper's Friends, who found him dumped in a bush next to the island's "kill cage." Ruban's parents, Anthony Gray and Alexis MacDonald, followed Sgt. Peppers Friends on social media and remember the day he was found; he was around six weeks old. About eight weeks later when he was ready for travel, the two welcomed him into their upstate New York home.

Robert "Prince Scratchabelly" Redfur is an eight-year-old miniature dachshund who grew up amid the hustle and bustle of New York City after his dads came and adopted him from a nice farmer in Princeton, New Jersey. He recently returned to his roots in the laid-back country when he moved upstate to Hudson, New York, with his family. "Robbie" adores Hudson Valley's black raspberry ice cream, but does not like the local fish (or seafood of any kind)!

Seamus and Samira are West Highland White Terriers who reside in the suburbs of New York City. When not modeling for dog craft books, Samira enjoys barking loudly as well as spending "alone time" in her crate. Seamus's interests include soft blankets, dog treats, and begging for raw vegetables. Together, this brother-sister pair often spend time outdoors chasing squirrels and going on walks with their humans.

Josie is an eight-year-old lab/Border collie mix. Although she may be gray around the muzzle, she can still run with the younger dogs and retrieve a tennis ball with the best of them. The Fine family adopted her from Animal Haven Shelter in New York City, and she now divides her time between Brooklyn and Long Island's North Fork.

Sharker adopted Kat's family in 2014. This small yet mighty Southern Belle has a mysterious past, though it's known that she lived in an animal shelter in Alabama before making her move to the Big Apple. She now enjoys filling her Brooklyn days with lots of naps and spying on the neighbors.

Resources

Below is a list of some great places to look if you are in need of supplies for the projects in this book. Many of the following stores have physical brick-and-mortar locations, but you can always simply shop online. Don't forget that your very own town may have some wonderful independent shops that also carry just what you need.

FABRIC

Mood
moodfabrics.com

JOANN Fabric and Craft Stores
joann.com

Fabric.com
fabric.com

GENERAL CRAFT

Michaels
michaels.com

A.C. Moore
acmoore.com

Etsy
etsy.com

CreateForLess
createforless.com

ART SUPPLIES

Artist & Craftsman Supply
artistcraftsman.com

Jerry's Artarama
jerrysartarama.com

Dick Blick
dickblick.com

HARDWARE SHOPS

Lowe's
lowes.com

Home Depot
homedepot.com

NOTIONS

Pacific Trimming
Pacifitrimming.com

M&J Trimming
mjtrims.com

PARTY SUPPLIES

Party City
partycity.com

Shindigz
shindigz.com

Party Glitters
partyglitter.com

Index

Note: Page numbers in *italics* indicate projects and templates.